Great Jobs

for

Computer Science Majors

Jan Goldberg

SERIES DEVELOPERS AND CONTRIBUTING AUTHORS
Stephen E. Lambert
Julie Ann DeGalan

VGM Career Horizons
NTC/Contemporary Publishing Company

Library of Congress Cataloging-in-Publication Data

Goldberg, Jan
    Great jobs for computer science majors / Jan Goldberg.
        p.   cm.
    ISBN 0-8442-4746-4
    1. Computer science—Vocational guidance. 2. Computer industry—
Employment. I. Title.
    QA76.25.G62 1997
    004'.023—dc21   97-21502
                                                  CIP

Dedication

To my husband, Larry,
for his continual love and support.

To my daughters, Sherri and Debbie,
for always believing in me.

And to the memory of my father and mother,
Sam and Sylvia Lefkovitz, for encouraging me
to follow my dreams.

Published by VGM Career Horizons
An imprint of NTC/Contemporary Publishing Company
4255 West Touhy Avenue, Lincolnwood (Chicago), Illinois 60646-1975 U.S.A.
Manufactured in the United States of America
International Standard Book Number: 0-8442-4746-4
15   14   13   12   11   10   9   8   7   6   5   4   3   2   1

CONTENTS

Acknowledgments   iv

Introduction   **Computer Science: A Degree That Will Take You Far**   v

PART ONE. THE JOB SEARCH   1

Chapter 1   **The Self-Assessment**   2

Chapter 2   **The Resume and Cover Letter**   22

Chapter 3   **Researching Careers**   44

Chapter 4   **Networking**   61

Chapter 5   **Interviewing**   74

Chapter 6   **Networking or Interviewing Follow-Up**   83

Chapter 7   **Job Offer Considerations**   88

Chapter 8   **The Graduate School Choice**   93

PART TWO. THE CAREER PATHS   105

Chapter 9   **Introduction to the Computer Science Career Paths**   106

Chapter 10   **Path 1: Computer Scientists and Systems Analysts**   109

Chapter 11   **Path 2: Management Analysts and Consultants**   134

Chapter 12   **Path 3: Operations Research Analysts**   147

Chapter 13   **Path 4: Computer Operators and Programmers**   155

Chapter 14   **Path 5: Computer Sales and Service**   170

Chapter 15   **Path 6: Other Computer Science Careers**   182

Appendix   **Colleges and Universities with Computer Science Programs**   200

Additional Resources   205

Index   210

Acknowledgments

The author gratefully acknowledges the professionals who graciously agreed to be profiled within and all of the associations and organizations that provided valuable and interesting information.

My dear husband, Larry; daughters, Sherri and Debbie; sister Adrienne; and brother, Paul, for their encouragement and support.

Family and close friends Bruce, Michele, Alison, Steven, Marty, Mindi, Cary, Michele, Marci, Steven, Brian, Jesse, Bertha, Aunt Estelle, Uncle Bernard, and Aunt Helen.

A special thanks to a special friend, Diana Catlin.

Sincere gratitude to Betsy Lancefield, my editor, for providing this challenging opportunity and help whenever and wherever it is needed.

COMPUTER SCIENCE: A DEGREE THAT WILL TAKE YOU FAR

"Any sufficiently advanced technology is indistinguishable from magic."

—Arthur C. Clarke, *The Lost Worlds of 2001*

Who built the first computer? The answer to this question depends on how you choose to define the word *computer*. The first mechanical calculating devices were created in the early seventeenth century. Though they could only perform a small number of mathematical functions (and sometimes not too well), they were the initial attempts at mechanizing the task of computation.

ANCIENT AND NOT-SO-ANCIENT HISTORY

Before the invention of calculating devices, astronomers, navigators, and scientists relied on books of tables for their calculations. These were completed by hand, typeset, and printed. Needless to say, calculations carried out by humans were subject to human error and the transcribing and typesetting produced additional errors. Thus, a new system had to be devised.

This was first attempted by great seventeenth-century mathematicians, such as Gottfried Wilhelm Leibniz and Blaise Pascal, whose mechanical calculators could perform the basic mathematical functions of addition, subtraction, multiplication, and division and could do so with speed and fairly good accuracy. However, there were still problems with the creation and use of these devices, such as difficulties in building them. While some improvements were made from these early designs, in truth computing machinery didn't show much improvement for almost 200 years.

In 1822, a young English astronomy student named Charles Babbage (1792–1871) authored a scientific paper called "On the Theoretical Principles of the Machinery for Calculating Tables," which included a proposal to construct a machine called the Difference Engine designed to mechanize the production of tables. Later Babbage changed his concept to an Analytical Engine which would be programmable. Babbage's ideas were well received by the Royal Astronomical Society, but circumstances prevented him from completing his project before his death in 1871. Though Babbage did not live to see it happen, he had a profound effect on computer technology. His use of punched cards as a storage device was 100 years ahead of its time, and the concepts of separate storage and computation units persist to this very day.

The next stage in the computer's evolution arrived in connection with the United States census of 1890. When the census was done in 1880, it took eight years to process and tabulate the data. To speed up this process, Herman Hollerith built an electromechanical unit that processed information on punched cards. The inventor used the punched cards to record information such as age, sex, nationality, and other vital statistics. While punched cards are no longer used in connection with computers, parts of Hollerith's code are still used to instruct computers on how to read input and format output.

The very first fully electronic calculator to compute complex equations was constructed by J. Presper Eckert and John W. Mauchly in the 1940s. The unit did speed up the solving of complex mathematical problems, but could not be programmed in the sense that we use that term today. Instead it had to be rewired by hand to solve new problems. And when one of its almost 18,000 vacuum tubes failed (which happened quite often), the system could not work properly.

This problem was largely overcome in 1948 by the transistor, which was developed by Bell Telephone Laboratories. With transistors, it was now possible to hand-wire basic operations into the computer itself, doing away with bulky and temperamental vacuum tubes and replacing them with smaller, more workable units.

A great contribution was made by mathematician-scientist John Von Neumann, whose concept of stored programs revolutionized the ease and speed with which a computer could be programmed. Von Neumann was responsible for defining the basic structure or design of the modern electronic digital computer.

Without the development of the semiconductor integrated circuit, however, the industry would undoubtedly have been confined to expensive specialized machines with only limited use.

During the 1950s, a process known as photolithography made it possible to print the wiring connecting circuit components much the same way that a photo can be printed from a negative. Distances between components were now greatly reduced. A few years later, researchers found a way to print the components themselves using a semiconductive material such as silicon. Now wiring and components could both be produced out of the same layer of semiconductive and other materials.

At that point, the computer industry was well on its way to becoming the great influence it now is in all aspects of modern life. Today, computers are at the center of continuing advances in technology. As a result, the demand for computer science graduates is soaring. As the workplace becomes more and more technology dependent, all types of employers are vying for in-house experts to keep their companies operating at peak efficiency. Computer science is a wide-open field that beckons to those who are interested and prepared. This is where you could take your place.

THE IMPORTANCE OF EDUCATION

To be competitive to prospective employers in the world of computers, it is very important to have a college degree—at least an undergraduate degree. This is the best way to ready yourself and to increase your chances in the job market. No matter what specific career you choose, a higher education will:

1. Offer a broad base of knowledge and experiences

2. Allow you to increase and perfect your skills

3. Provide you with opportunities to gain important personal and professional contacts

4. Give you the knowledge you need to make an informed career decision

Because there is intense competition in the job market, with a multitude of talented, dedicated people vying for each job opening, you must always seek to set yourself above and apart from others. A dynamite combination is a college degree with at least one internship, additional formal training or study, and experience working in the field. That's the way to truly position yourself with an edge over other well-qualified candidates.

Good luck in your quest!

PART ONE

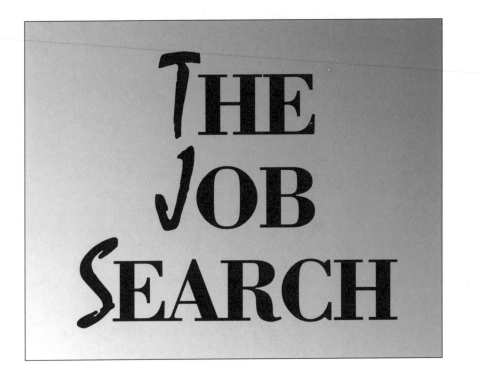

THE JOB SEARCH

CHAPTER ONE

THE
SELF-ASSESSMENT

elf-assessment is the process by which you begin to acknowledge your own particular blend of education, experiences, values, needs, and goals. It provides the foundation for career planning and the entire job search process. Self-assessment involves looking inward and asking yourself what can sometimes prove to be difficult questions. This self-examination should lead to an intimate understanding of your personal traits, your personal values, your consumption patterns and economic needs, your longer-term goals, your skill base, your preferred skills, and your underdeveloped skills.

You come to the self-assessment process knowing yourself well in some of these areas, but you may still be uncertain about other aspects. You may be well aware of your consumption patterns, but have you spent much time specifically identifying your longer-term goals, or your personal values as they relate to work? No matter what level of self-assessment you have undertaken to date, it is now time to clarify all of these issues and questions as they relate to the job search.

The knowledge you gain in the self-assessment process will guide the rest of your job search. In this book, you will learn about all of the following tasks:

- ❑ Writing resumes

- ❑ Exploring possible job titles

- ❑ Identifying employment sites

- ❑ Networking

- ❑ Interviewing

- ❑ Following up

- ❑ Evaluating job offers

In each of these steps, you will rely on and return often to the understanding gained through your self-assessment. Any individual seeking employment must be able and willing to express to potential recruiters and interviewers throughout the job search these facets of his or her personality. This communication allows you to show the world who you are so that together with employers you can determine whether there will be a workable match with a given job or career path.

How to Conduct a Self-Assessment

The self-assessment process goes on naturally all the time. People ask you to clarify what you mean, or you make a purchasing decision, or you begin a new relationship. You react to the world and the world reacts to you. How you understand these interactions and any changes you might make because of them are part of the natural process of self-discovery. There is, however, a more comprehensive and efficient way to approach self-assessment with regard to employment.

Because self-assessment can become a complex exercise, we have distilled it into a seven-step process that provides an effective basis for undertaking a job search. The seven steps include the following:

1. Understanding your personal traits

2. Identifying your personal values

3. Calculating your economic needs

4. Exploring your longer-term goals

5. Enumerating your skill base

6. Recognizing your preferred skills

7. Assessing skills needing further development

As you work through your self-assessment, you might want to create a worksheet similar to the one shown in Exhibit 1.1. Or you might want to keep a journal of the thoughts you have as you undergo this process. There will be many opportunities to revise your self-assessment as you start down the path of seeking a career.

STEP 1 Understanding Your Personal Traits

Each person has a unique personality that he or she brings to the job search process. Gaining a better understanding of your personal traits can help you evaluate job and career choices. Identifying these traits, then finding employment that allows you to draw on at least some of them can create a rewarding and fulfilling work experience. If potential employment doesn't allow you to use these preferred traits, it is important to decide whether you can find other ways to express them or

Exhibit 1.1

Self-Assessment Worksheet

STEP 1. Understand Your Personal Traits
The personal traits that describe me are:
(Include all of the words that describe you.)

The ten personal traits that most accurately describe me are:
(List these ten traits.)

STEP 2. Identify Your Personal Values
Working conditions that are important to me include:
(List working conditions that would have to exist for you to accept a position.)

The values that go along with my working conditions are:
(Write down the values that correspond to each working condition.)

Some additional values I've decided to include are:
(List those values you identify as you conduct this job search.)

STEP 3. Calculate Your Economic Needs
My estimated minimum annual salary requirement is:
(Write the salary you have calculated based on your budget.)

Starting salaries for the positions I'm considering are:
(List the name of each job you are considering and the associated starting salary.)

STEP 4. Explore Your Longer-Term Goals
My thoughts on longer-term goals right now are:
(Jot down some of your longer-term goals as you know them right now.)

continued

continued

STEP 5. Enumerate Your Skill Base

The general skills I possess are:
(List the skills that underlie tasks you are able to complete.)

The specific skills I possess are:
(List more technical or specific skills that you possess and indicate your level of expertise.)

General and specific skills that I want to promote to employers for the jobs I'm considering are:
(List general and specific skills for each type of job you are considering.)

STEP 6. Recognize Your Preferred Skills

Skills that I would like to use on the job include:
(List skills that you hope to use on the job, and indicate how often you'd like to use them.)

STEP 7. Assess Skills Needing Further Development

Some skills that I'll need to acquire for the jobs I'm considering include:
(Write down skills listed in job advertisements or job descriptions that you don't currently possess.)

I believe I can build these skills by:
(Describe how you plan to acquire these skills.)

whether you would be better off not considering this type of job. Interests and hobbies pursued outside of work hours can be one way to use personal traits you don't have an opportunity to draw on in your work. For example, if you consider yourself an outgoing person and the kinds of jobs you are examining allow little contact with other people, you may be able to achieve the level of interaction that is comfortable for you outside of your work setting. If such a compromise seems impractical or otherwise unsatisfactory, you probably should explore only jobs that provide the interaction you want and need on the job.

Many young adults who are not very confident about their attractiveness to employers will downplay their need for income. They will say, "Money is not all that important if I love my work." But if you begin to document exactly what you need for housing, transportation, insurance, clothing, food, and utilities, you will begin to understand that some jobs cannot meet your financial needs and it doesn't matter how wonderful the job is. If you have to worry each payday about bills and other financial obligations, you won't be very effective on the job. Begin now to be honest with yourself about your needs.

Inventorying Your Personal Traits. Begin the self-assessment process by creating an inventory of your personal traits. Using the list in Exhibit 1.2, decide which of these personal traits describe you.

Exhibit 1.2

Personal Traits

Accurate	Critical	Generous
Active	Curious	Gentle
Adaptable	Daring	Good-natured
Adventurous	Decisive	Helpful
Affectionate	Deliberate	Honest
Aggressive	Detail-oriented	Humorous
Ambitious	Determined	Idealistic
Analytical	Discreet	Imaginative
Appreciative	Dominant	Impersonal
Artistic	Eager	Independent
Brave	Easygoing	Individualistic
Businesslike	Efficient	Industrious
Calm	Emotional	Informal
Capable	Empathetic	Innovative
Caring	Energetic	Intellectual
Cautious	Excitable	Intelligent
Cheerful	Expressive	Introverted
Clean	Extroverted	Intuitive
Competent	Fair-minded	Inventive
Confident	Farsighted	Jovial
Conscientious	Feeling	Just
Conservative	Firm	Kind
Considerate	Flexible	Liberal
Cool	Formal	Likable
Cooperative	Friendly	Logical
Courageous	Future-oriented	

continued

continued

Loyal	Precise	Serious
Mature	Principled	Sincere
Methodical	Private	Sociable
Meticulous	Productive	Spontaneous
Mistrustful	Progressive	Strong
Modest	Quick	Strong-minded
Motivated	Quiet	Structured
Objective	Rational	Subjective
Observant	Realistic	Tactful
Open-minded	Receptive	Thorough
Opportunistic	Reflective	Thoughtful
Optimistic	Relaxed	Tolerant
Organized	Reliable	Trusting
Original	Reserved	Trustworthy
Outgoing	Resourceful	Truthful
Patient	Responsible	Understanding
Peaceable	Reverent	Unexcitable
Personable	Sedentary	Uninhibited
Persuasive	Self-confident	Verbal
Pleasant	Self-controlled	Versatile
Poised	Self-disciplined	Wholesome
Polite	Sensible	Wise
Practical	Sensitive	

Focusing on Selected Personal Traits.   Of all the traits you identified from the list in Exhibit 1.2, select the ten you believe most accurately describe you. If you are having a difficult time deciding, think about which words people who know you well would use to describe you. Keep track of these ten traits.

Considering Your Personal Traits in the Job Search Process.   As you begin exploring jobs and careers, watch for matches between your personal traits and the job descriptions you read. Some jobs will require many personal traits you know you possess, and others will not seem to match those traits.

....

> A systems analyst, for example, doing consulting work for large corporations, must interact with a range of personnel in various departments. He or she must have the ability to coordinate the schedules and activities of various workers and supervisors. Excellent organizational and interpersonal skills

are essential for someone in this position. But a freelance software designer usually works alone, with limited opportunities to interact with others. Both often have deadlines to meet, but the software designer has far fewer people to answer to and must be able to work independently.

···

Your ability to respond to changing conditions, decision-making ability, productivity, creativity, and verbal skills all have a bearing on your success in and enjoyment of your work life. To better guarantee success, be sure to take the time needed to understand these traits in yourself.

STEP 2   Identifying Your Personal Values

Your personal values affect every aspect of your life, including employment, and they develop and change as you move through life. Values can be defined as principles that we hold in high regard, qualities that are important and desirable to us. Some values aren't ordinarily connected to work (love, beauty, color, light, marriage, family, or religion), and others are (autonomy, cooperation, effectiveness, achievement, knowledge, and security). Our values determine, in part, the level of satisfaction we feel in a particular job.

Defining Acceptable Working Conditions.   One facet of employment is the set of working conditions that must exist for someone to consider taking a job.

Each of us would probably create a unique list of acceptable working conditions, but items that might be included on many people's lists are the amount of money you would need to be paid, how far you are willing to drive or travel, the amount of freedom you want in determining your own schedule, whether you would be working with people or data or things, and the types of tasks you would be willing to do. Your conditions might include statements of working conditions you will *not* accept; for example, you might not be willing to work at night or on weekends or holidays.

If you were offered a job tomorrow, what conditions would have to exist for you to realistically consider accepting the position? Take some time and make a list of these conditions.

Realizing Associated Values.   Your list of working conditions can be used to create an inventory of your values relating to jobs and careers you are exploring. For example, if one of your conditions stated that you wanted to earn at least $25,000 per year, the associated value would be financial gain. If another condition was that you wanted to work with a friendly group of people, the value that goes along with

---

Exhibit 1.3

Work Values

Achievement	Development	Physical activity
Advancement	Effectiveness	Power
Adventure	Excitement	Precision
Attainment	Fast pace	Prestige
Authority	Financial gain	Privacy
Autonomy	Helping	Profit
Belonging	Humor	Recognition
Challenge	Improvisation	Risk
Change	Independence	Security
Communication	Influencing others	Self-expression
Community	Intellectual stimulation	Solitude
Competition	Interaction	Stability
Completion	Knowledge	Status
Contribution	Leading	Structure
Control	Mastery	Supervision
Cooperation	Mobility	Surroundings
Creativity	Moral fulfillment	Time freedom
Decision-making	Organization	Variety

---

that might be belonging or interaction with people. Exhibit 1.3 provides a list of commonly held values that relate to the work environment; use it to create your own list of personal values.

Relating Your Values to the World of Work. As you read the job descriptions in this book and in other suggested resources, think about the values associated with that position.

· ·

For example, in computer sales, your duties may include calling on clients; explaining products and/or services you offer; arranging delivery; and/or installing and providing follow-up services after the sale. Associated qualities include knowledge, mastery, competition, and variety.

· ·

If you were thinking about a career in this field, or any other field you're exploring, at least some of the associated values should match those you extracted from your list of working conditions. Take a second look at any values that don't match up. How important are they to you? What will happen if they are not satisfied on the job? Can you incorporate those personal values elsewhere? Your answers need to be brutally honest. As you continue your exploration, be sure to add to your list any additional values that occur to you.

STEP 3 Calculating Your Economic Needs

Each of us grew up in an environment that provided for certain basic needs, such as food and shelter, and, to varying degrees, other needs that we now consider basic, such as cable TV, reading materials, or an automobile. Needs such as privacy, space, and quiet, which at first glance may not appear to be monetary needs, may add to housing expenses and so should be considered as you examine your economic needs. For example, if you place a high value on a large, open living space for yourself, it would be difficult to satisfy that need without an associated high housing cost, especially in a densely populated city environment.

As you prepare to move into the world of work and become responsible for meeting your own basic needs, it is important to consider the salary you will need to be able to afford a satisfying standard of living. The three-step process outlined here will help you plan a budget, which in turn will allow you to evaluate the various career choices and geographic locations you are considering. The steps include (1) developing a realistic budget, (2) examining starting salaries, and (3) using a cost-of-living index.

Developing a Realistic Budget.   Each of us has certain expectations for the kind of lifestyle we want to maintain. In order to begin the process of defining your economic needs, it will be helpful to determine what you expect to spend on routine monthly expenses. These expenses include housing, food, transportation, entertainment, utilities, loan repayments, and revolving charge accounts. A worksheet that details many of these expenses is shown in Exhibit 1.4. You may not currently spend for certain items, but you probably will have to once you begin supporting yourself. As you develop this budget, be generous in your estimates, but keep in mind any items that could be

---

Exhibit 1.4

Estimated Monthly Expenses Worksheet

		Could Reduce Spending? (Yes/No)
Cable	$ _____	_____
Child care	_____	_____
Clothing	_____	_____

continued

continued

		Could Reduce Spending? (Yes/No)
Educational loan repayment	_____	_____
Entertainment	_____	_____
Food	_____	_____
At home	_____	_____
Meals out	_____	_____
Gifts	_____	_____
Housing		
Rent/mortgage	_____	_____
Insurance	_____	_____
Property taxes	_____	_____
Medical insurance	_____	_____
Reading materials		
Newspapers	_____	_____
Magazines	_____	_____
Books	_____	_____
Revolving loans/charges	_____	_____
Savings	_____	_____
Telephone	_____	_____
Transportation		
Auto payment	_____	_____
Insurance	_____	_____
Parking	_____	_____
—or		
Cab/train/bus fare	_____	_____
Utilities		
Electric	_____	_____
Gas	_____	_____
Water/sewer	_____	_____
Vacations	_____	_____
Miscellaneous expense 1	_____	_____
Expense: _____		
Miscellaneous expense 2	_____	_____
Expense: _____		
Miscellaneous expense 3	_____	_____
Expense: _____		

TOTAL MONTHLY EXPENSES: _____

YEARLY EXPENSES (Monthly expenses x 12): _____

INCREASE TO INCLUDE TAXES (Yearly expenses x 1.35): _____ =
MINIMUM ANNUAL SALARY REQUIREMENT ___ _____

reduced or eliminated. If you are not sure about the cost of a certain item, talk with family or friends who would be able to give you a realistic estimate.

If this is new or difficult for you, start to keep a log of expenses right now. You may be surprised at how much you actually spend each month for food or stamps or magazines. Household expenses and personal grooming items can often loom very large in a budget, as can auto repairs or home maintenance.

Income taxes must also be taken into consideration when examining salary requirements. State and local taxes vary by location, so it is difficult to calculate exactly the effect of taxes on the amount of income you need to generate. To roughly estimate the gross income necessary to generate your minimum annual salary requirement, multiply the minimum salary you have calculated (see Exhibit 1.4) by a factor of 1.35. The resulting figure will be an approximation of what your gross income would need to be, given your estimated expenses.

Examining Starting Salaries.　Starting salaries for each of the career tracks are provided throughout this book. These salary figures can be used in conjunction with the cost-of-living index (discussed in the next section) to determine whether you would be able to meet your basic economic needs in a given geographic location.

Using a Cost-of-Living Index.　If you are thinking about trying to get a job in a geographic region other than the one where you now live, understanding differences in the cost of living will help you come to a more informed decision about making a move. By using a cost-of-living index, you can compare salaries offered and the cost of living in different locations with what you know about the salaries offered and the cost of living in your present location.

Many variables are used to calculate the cost-of-living index, including housing expenses, groceries, utilities, transportation, health care, clothing, entertainment, local income taxes, and local sales taxes. Cost-of-living indices can be found in many resources, such as *Equal Employment Opportunity Bimonthly*, *Places Rated Almanac*, or *The Best Towns in America*. They are constantly being recalculated based on changes in costs.

....

If you lived in Cleveland, Ohio, for example, and you were interested in working as a sales representative for a computer firm, you would earn, on average, $20,784 annually. But let's say you're also thinking about moving to either New York, Los Angeles, or Denver. You know you can live on $20,784 in Cleveland, but you want to be able to equate that salary in other locations you're considering.

How much will you need to earn in those locations to do this? Figuring the cost of living for each city will show you.

Let's walk through this example. In any cost-of-living index, the number 100 represents the national average cost of living, and each city is assigned an index number based on current prices in that city for the items included in the index (housing, food, etc.). In the index we used, New York was assigned the number 213.3, Los Angeles' index was 124.6, Denver's was 100.0, and Cleveland's index was 114.3. In other words, it costs more than twice as much to live in New York as it does in Denver. We can set up a table to determine exactly how much you would have to earn in each of these cities to have the same buying power that you have in Cleveland.

Job: Sales Representative

CITY	INDEX	EQUIVALENT SALARY

$$\frac{\text{New York} \quad 213.3}{\text{Cleveland} \quad 114.3} \times \$20{,}784 = \$38{,}785 \text{ in New York}$$

$$\frac{\text{Los Angeles} \quad 124.6}{\text{Cleveland} \quad 114.3} \times \$20{,}784 = \$22{,}656 \text{ in Los Angeles}$$

$$\frac{\text{Denver} \quad 100.0}{\text{Cleveland} \quad 114.3} \times \$20{,}784 = \$18{,}199 \text{ in Denver}$$

You would have to earn $38,785 in New York, $22,656 in Los Angeles, and $18,199 in Denver to match the buying power of $20,784 in Cleveland.

If you would like to determine whether it's financially worthwhile to make any of these moves, one more piece of information is needed: the salaries of sales representatives in these other cities. The *American Salaries and Wages Survey* (3rd edition, 1995) reports the following average salary information for sales representatives in their 1995 salary survey:

Region	Annual Salary	Salary Equivalent to Ohio	Change in Buying Power
Mid-Atlantic (including New York)	$29,030	$38,785	−$9,755
West (including Los Angeles)	$23,070	$22,656	+$ 414
Mountain Plains (including Denver)	$22,862	$18,199	+$3,863
Midwest (including Cleveland)	$20,784	—	—

If you moved to New York City and secured employment as a sales representative for a computer firm, you would not be able to maintain a lifestyle similar to the one you led in Cleveland; in fact, you would have to add more than fifty percent to your income to maintain a similar lifestyle in New York. The same would not be true for a move to Los Angeles or Denver. You would increase your buying power given the rate of pay and cost of living in these cities.

....

You can work through a similar exercise for any type of job you are considering and for many locations when current salary information is available. It will be worth your time to undertake this analysis if you are seriously considering a relocation. By doing so you will be able to make an informed choice.

STEP 4 Exploring Your Longer-Term Goals

There is no question that when we first begin working, our goals are to use our skills and education in a job that will reward us with employment, income, and status relative to the preparation we brought with us to this position. If we are not being paid as much as we feel we should for our level of education, or if job demands don't provide the intellectual stimulation we had hoped for, we experience unhappiness and, as a result, often seek other employment.

Most jobs we consider "good" are those that fulfill our basic "lower-level" needs of security, food, clothing, shelter, income, and productive work. But even when our basic needs are met and our jobs are secure and productive, we as individuals are constantly changing. As we change, the demands and expectations we place on our jobs may change. Fortunately, some jobs grow and change with us, and this explains why some people are happy throughout many years in a job.

But more often people are bigger than the jobs they fill. We have more goals and needs than any job could fulfill. These are "higher-level" needs of self-esteem, companionship, affection, and an increasing desire to feel we are employing our-selves in the most effective way possible. Not all of these higher-level needs can be fulfilled through employment, but for as long as we are employed, we increasingly demand that our jobs play their part in moving us along the path to fulfillment.

Another obvious but important fact is that we change as we mature. Although our jobs also have the potential for change, they may not change as frequently or as markedly as we do. There are increasingly fewer one-job, one-employer careers; we must think about a work future that may involve voluntary or forced moves from employer to employer. Because of that very real possibility, we need to take advantage of the opportunities in each position we hold to acquire skills and competencies that will keep us viable and attractive as employees in a job market that is not only increasingly technology/computer dependent, but also is populated with more and more small, self-transforming organizations rather than the large, seemingly stable organizations of the past.

It may be difficult in the early stages of the job search to determine whether the path you are considering can meet these longer-term goals. Reading about career paths and individual career histories in your field can be very helpful in this regard. Meeting and talking with individuals further along in their careers can be enlightening as well. Older workers can provide valuable guidance on "self-managing" your career, which will become an increasingly valuable skill in the future. Some of these ideas may seem remote as you read this now, but you should be able to appreciate the need to ensure that you are growing, developing valuable new skills, and researching other employers who might be interested in your particular skills package.

· ·

If you are considering a position in retail computer sales, you would gain a better perspective on this career if you talked to an entry-level associate buyer, a more experienced associate or department head, and finally a vice president for sales merchandising or store operations who has a considerable work history in the retail sector. Each will have a different perspective, unique concerns, and an individual set of value priorities.

· ·

STEP 5   Enumerating Your Skill Base

In terms of the job search, skills can be thought of as capabilities that can be developed in school, at work, or by volunteering and then used in specific job settings. Many studies have documented the kinds of skills that employers seek in entry-level applicants. For example, some of the most desired skills for individuals interested in the teaching profession include the ability to interact effectively with students one on one, to manage a classroom, to adapt to varying situations as necessary, and to get involved in school activities. Business employers have also identified important qualities, including enthusiasm for the employer's product or service, a businesslike mind, the ability to follow written or verbal instructions, the ability to demonstrate self-control, the confidence to suggest new ideas, the ability to communicate with all members of a group, awareness of cultural differences, and loyalty, to name just a few. You will find that many of these skills are also in the repertoire of qualities demanded in your college major.

In order to be successful in obtaining any given job, you must be able to demonstrate that you possess a certain mix of skills that will allow you to carry out the duties required by that job. This skill mix will vary a great deal from job to job; to determine the skills necessary for the jobs you are seeking, you can read job advertisements or more generic job descriptions, such as those found later in this book. If you want to be effective in the job search, you must directly show employers that you possess the skills needed to be successful in filling the position. These skills will initially be described on your resume and then discussed again during the interview process.

Skills are either general or specific. General skills are those that are developed throughout the college years by taking classes, being employed, and getting involved in other related activities such as volunteer work or campus organizations. General skills include the ability to read and write, to perform computations, to think critically, and to communicate effectively. Specific skills are also acquired on the job and in the classroom, but they allow you to complete tasks that require specialized knowledge. Computer programming, drafting, language translating, and copyediting are just a few examples of specific skills that may relate to a given job.

In order to develop a list of skills relevant to employers, you must first identify the general skills you possess, then list specific skills you have to offer, and, finally, examine which of these skills employers are seeking.

Identifying Your General Skills.   Because you possess or will possess a college degree, employers will assume that you can read and write, perform certain basic computations, think critically, and communicate effectively. Employers will want to see that you have acquired these skills, and they will want to know which additional general skills you possess.

One way to begin identifying skills is to write an experiential diary. An experiential diary lists all the tasks you were responsible for completing for each job you've held and then outlines the skills required to do those tasks. You may list several skills for any given task. This diary allows you to distinguish between the tasks you performed and the underlying skills required to complete those tasks. Here's an example:

Tasks	Skills
Answering telephone	Effective use of language, clear diction, ability to direct inquiries, ability to solve problems
Waiting on tables	Poise under conditions of time and pressure, speed, accuracy, good memory, simultaneous completion of tasks, sales skills

For each job or experience you have participated in, develop a worksheet based on the example shown here. On a resume, you may want to describe these skills rather than simply listing tasks. Skills are easier for the employer to appreciate, especially when your experience is very different from the employment you are seeking. In addition to helping you identify general skills, this experiential diary will prepare you to speak more effectively in an interview about the qualifications you possess.

Identifying Your Specific Skills.   It may be easier to identify your specific skills, because you can definitely say whether you can speak other languages, program a computer, draft a map or diagram, or edit a document using appropriate symbols and terminology.

Using your experiential diary, identify the points in your history where you learned how to do something very specific, and decide whether you have a beginning, intermediate, or advanced knowledge of how to use that particular skill. Right now, be sure to list *every* specific skill you have, and don't consider whether you like using the skill. Write down a list of specific skills you have acquired and the level of competence you possess—beginning, intermediate, or advanced.

Relating Your Skills to Employers.   You probably have thought about a couple of different jobs you might be interested in obtaining, and one way to begin relating the general and specific skills you possess to potential employer needs is to read actual advertisements for these types of positions (see Part II for resources listing actual job openings).

··

For example, you might be interested in a career as a computer engineer. A typical job listing might read, "Requires 2–5 years experience, organizational and interpersonal skills, and the ability to work under pressure." If you then used any one of a number of general sources of information that describes the job of a computer engineer, you would find additional information. Computer engineers also work with the hardware and software aspects of system design and development; they may be involved with the design of new computing devices or computer-related equipment; they must be able both to work as part of a team and to function independently, depending on the job setting; and finally, they must also keep abreast of rapidly occurring advances in the field.

Begin building a comprehensive list of required skills with the first job description you read. Exploring advertisements for and descriptions of several types of related positions will reveal an important core of skills necessary for obtaining the type of work you're interested in. In building this list, include both general and specific skills.

Following is a sample list of skills needed to be successful as a computer engineer. These items were extracted from general resources and actual job listings.

Job: Computer Engineer

General Skills	Specific Skills
Gather information	Test computer designs
Have a specific body of knowledge	Be familiar with CASE tools
Pay attention to detail	Write memos
Present technical knowledge in laymen's terms	Be familiar with uses of virtual reality
Work well with other people	Prepare specifications
Be organized	Create structural diagrams
Perform several tasks simultaneously	Write reports
Be able to supervise the work of others	Be familiar with object-oriented programming languages

---

On separate sheets of paper, try to generate a comprehensive list of required skills for at least one job you are considering.

> The list of general skills that you develop for a given career path would be valuable for any number of jobs you might apply for. Many of the specific skills would also be transferable to other types of positions. For example, possessing expertise in Computer-Aided Software Engineering (CASE) would be a required skill for computer engineers, and it would also be a required skill for systems analysts.
>
> ....

Now review the list of skills you developed and check off those skills that *you know you possess* and that are required for jobs you are considering. You should refer to these specific skills on the resume that you write for this type of job. See Chapter 2 for details on resume writing.

STEP 6   Recognizing Your Preferred Skills

In the previous section, you developed a comprehensive list of skills that relate to particular career paths that are of interest to you. You can now relate these to skills that you prefer to use. We all use a wide range of skills (some researchers say individuals have a repertoire of about 500 skills), but we may not be particularly interested in using all of them in our work. There may be some skills that come to us more naturally or that we use successfully time and time again and that we want to continue to use; these are best described as our preferred skills. For this exercise, use the list of skills that you developed for the previous section and decide which of them you are *most interested in using* in future work and how often you would like to use them. You might be interested in using some skills only occasionally, while others you would like to use more regularly. You probably also have skills that you hope you can use constantly.

As you examine job announcements, look for matches between this list of preferred skills and the qualifications described in the advertisements. These skills should be highlighted on your resume and discussed in job interviews.

STEP 7   Assessing Skills Needing Further Development

Previously you developed a list of general and specific skills required for given positions. You already possess some of these skills; those that remain to be developed are your underdeveloped skills.

If you are just beginning the job search, there may be gaps between the qualifications required for some of the jobs being considered and skills you possess. These are your underdeveloped skills. The thought of having to admit to and talk about these underdeveloped skills, especially in a job interview, is a frightening one. One way to put a healthy perspective on this subject is to target and relate your exploration of underdeveloped skills to the types of positions you are seeking. Recognizing these shortcomings and planning to overcome them with either on-the-job training or additional formal education can be a positive way to address the concept of underdeveloped skills.

On your worksheet or in your journal, make a list of up to five general or specific skills required for the positions you're interested in that you *don't currently possess.* For each item, list an idea you have for specific action you could take to acquire that skill. Do some brainstorming to come up with possible actions. If you have a hard time generating ideas, talk to people currently working in this type of position, professionals in your college career services office, trusted friends, family members, or members of related professional associations.

If, for example, you are interested in a job for which you don't have some specific required experience, you could locate training opportunities such as classes or workshops offered through a local college or university, community college, or club or association that would help you build the level of expertise you need for the job.

Many excellent jobs in today's economy demand computer skills you probably already have. Most graduates are not so lucky, and have to acquire these skills—often before an employer will give their applications serious consideration. So, what can you do if you find there are certain skills you're missing? If you're still in school, try to fill the gaps in your knowledge before you graduate. If you've already graduated, look at evening programs, continuing education courses, or tutorial programs that may be available commercially. Developing a modest level of expertise will encourage you to be more confident in suggesting to potential employers that you can continue to add to your skill base on the job.

In Chapter 5 on interviewing, we will discuss in detail how to effectively address questions about underdeveloped skills. Generally speaking, though, employers want genuine answers to these types of questions. They want you to reveal "the real you," and they also want to see how you answer difficult questions. In taking the positive, targeted approach discussed above, you show the employer that you are willing to continue to learn and that you have a plan for strengthening your job qualifications.

USING YOUR SELF-ASSESSMENT

Exploring entry-level career options can be an exciting experience if you have good resources available and will take the time to use them. Can you effectively complete the following tasks?

1. Understand and relate your personality traits to career choices

2. Define your personal values

3. Determine your economic needs

4. Explore longer-term goals

5. Understand your skill base

6. Recognize your preferred skills

7. Express a willingness to improve on your underdeveloped skills

If so, then you can more meaningfully participate in the job search process by writing a more effective resume, finding job titles that represent work you are interested in doing, locating job sites that will provide the opportunity for you to use your strengths and skills, networking in an informed way, participating in focused interviews, getting the most out of follow-up contacts, and evaluating job offers to find those that create a good match between you and the employer. The remaining chapters guide you through these next steps in the job search process. For many job seekers, this process can take anywhere from three months to a year to implement. The time you will need to put into your job search will depend on the type of job you want and the geographic location where you'd like to work. Think of your effort as a job in itself, requiring you to set aside time each week to complete the needed work. Carefully undertaken efforts may reduce the time you need for your job search.

CHAPTER TWO

THE RESUME AND COVER LETTER

he task of writing a resume may seem overwhelming if you are unfamiliar with this type of document, but there are some easily understood techniques that can and should be used. This section was written to help you understand the purpose of the resume, the different types of resume formats available, and how to write the sections of information traditionally found on a resume. We will present examples and explanations that address questions frequently posed by people writing their first resume or updating an old resume.

Even within the formats and suggestions given below, however, there are infinite variations. True, most resumes follow one of the outlines suggested below, but you should feel free to adjust the resume to suit your needs and make it expressive of your life and experience.

WHY WRITE A RESUME?

The purpose of a resume is to convince an employer that you should be interviewed. You'll want to present enough information to show that you can make an immediate and valuable contribution to an organization. A resume is not an in-depth historical or legal document; later in the job search process you'll be asked to document your entire work history on an application form and attest to its validity. The resume should, instead, highlight relevant information pertaining directly to the organization that will receive the document or the type of position you are seeking.

We will discuss four types of resumes in this chapter: chronological resume, functional resume, targeted resume, and the broadcast letter. The reasons for using one type of resume over another and the typical format for each are addressed in the following sections.

THE CHRONOLOGICAL RESUME

The chronological resume is the most common of the various resume formats and therefore the format that employers are most used to receiving. This type of resume is easy to read and understand because it details the chronological progression of jobs you have held. (See Exhibit 2.1.) It begins with your most recent employment and works back in time. If you have a solid work history, or experience that provided growth and development in your duties and responsibilities, a chronological resume will highlight these achievements. The typical elements of a chronological resume include the heading, a career objective, educational background, employment experience, activities, and references.

The Heading

The heading consists of your name, address, and telephone number. Recently it has come to include fax numbers and electronic mail addresses as well. We suggest that you spell out your full name and type it in all capital letters in bold type. After all, *you* are the focus of the resume! If you have a current as well a permanent address and you include both in the heading, be sure to indicate until what date your current address will be valid. The two-letter state abbreviation should be the only abbreviation that appears in your heading. Don't forget to include the zip code with your address and the area code with your telephone number.

The Objective

As you formulate the wording for this part of your resume, keep the following points in mind.

The Objective Focuses the Resume.
Without a doubt, this is the most challenging part of the resume for most resume writers. Even for individuals who have quite firmly decided on a career path, it can be difficult to encapsulate all they want to say in one or two brief sentences. For job seekers who are unfocused or unclear about their intentions, trying to write this section can inhibit the entire resume writing process.

Recruiters tell us, time and again, that the objective creates a frame of reference for them. It helps them see how you express your goals and career focus. In

Exhibit 2.1

Chronological Resume

MARSHALL EVANS

Linton Hall #346	3220 Sebastian
University of California	Montreal, P.Q.
Santa Cruz, CA 95060	H3H 1H9
(408) 555-2331	Canada
(until September 1997)	(514) 555-4550

OBJECTIVE
A career as a computer games software designer for a major manufacturer, ultimately moving into management.

EDUCATION
Bachelor of Science in Computer Science
University of California
Santa Cruz, California
September 1997

RELATED COURSES

Database Management	Research Design
Business Systems Design	Personnel Management
Real Estate Investment	Labor Relations

EXPERIENCE
Self-Employed
Designed and self-marketed *Vaders,* computer action game
1996 to present

Internship
Computer Support Analyst
America Online
Provided technical assistance to America Online members; worked with other technicians and AOL full-time staff to troubleshoot system problems
1995 to Present

continued

---

continued

Part-time Summers
Computer Sales
CompUSA, Santa Cruz, California
Direct floor sales, providing assistance to customers and
answering questions related to various hardware and software
1994 to 1996

PORTFOLIO
Portfolio of my computer games completed during the last two years
is available upon request.

REFERENCES
Both personal and professional references are available upon
request.

---

addition, the statement may indicate in what ways you can immediately benefit an organization. Given the importance of the objective, every point covered in the resume should relate to it. If information doesn't relate, it should be omitted. With the word processing technology available today, each resume can and should be tailored for individual employers or specific positions that are available.

Choose an Appropriate Length.   Because of the brevity necessary for a resume, you should keep the objective as short as possible. Although objectives of only four or five words often don't show much direction, objectives that take three full lines would be viewed as too wordy and might possibly be ignored.

Consider Which Type of Objective Statement You Will Use.   There are many ways to state an objective, but generally there are four forms this statement can take: (1) a very general statement; (2) a statement focused on a specific position; (3) a statement focused on a specific industry; or (4) a summary of your qualifications. In our contacts with employers, we often hear that many resumes don't exhibit any direction or career goals, so we suggest avoiding general statements when possible.

1. General Objective Statement.   General objective statements look like the following:

❑ An entry-level educational programming coordinator position

❑ An entry-level marketing position

This type of objective would be useful if you know what type of job you want but you're not sure which industries interest you.

2. Position-Focused Objective. Following are examples of objectives focusing on a specific position:

- ❏ To obtain the position of Conference Coordinator at State College

- ❏ To obtain a position as Assistant Editor at *Time* magazine

When a student applies for an advertised job opening, this type of focus can be very effective. The employer knows that the applicant has taken the time to tailor the resume specifically for this position.

3. Industry-Focused Objective. Focusing on a particular industry in an objective could be stated as follows:

- ❏ To begin a career as a sales representative in the cruise line industry

4. Summary of Qualifications Statement. The summary of qualifications can be used instead of an objective or in conjunction with an objective. The purpose of this type of statement is to highlight relevant qualifications gained through a variety of experiences. This type of statement is often used by individuals with extensive and diversified work experience. An example of a qualifications statement follows:

··

A degree in computer science and three years of progressively increasing responsibilities in the financial department of a national bank as an applications programmer have prepared me for a career in an institution that values hands-on involvement and thoroughness.

··

Support Your Objective. A resume that contains any one of these types of objective statements should then go on to demonstrate why you are qualified to get the position. Listing academic degrees can be one way to indicate qualifications. Another demonstration would be in the way previous experiences, both volunteer and paid, are described. Without this kind of documentation in the body of the resume, the objective looks unsupported. Think of the resume as telling a connected story about you. All the elements should work together to form a coherent picture that ideally should relate to your statement of objective.

Education

This section of your resume should indicate the exact name of the degree you will receive or have received, spelled out completely with no abbreviations.

The degree is generally listed after the objective, followed by the institution name and address, and then the month and year of graduation. This section could also include your academic minor, grade point average (GPA), and appearance on the Dean's List or President's List.

If you have enough space, you might want to include a section listing courses related to the field in which you are seeking work. The best use of a "related courses" section would be to list some course work that is not traditionally associated with the major. Perhaps you took several computer courses outside your degree that will be helpful and related to the job prospects you are entertaining. Several education section examples are shown here:

· ·

❑ Bachelor of Science degree in Computer Science
Northeastern University, Boston, Massachusetts, May 1997
Minor: Accounting

❑ Bachelor of Science degree in Computer Science
Tufts University, Medford, Massachusetts, May 1997
Minor: Mathematics

❑ Bachelor of Science degree in Computer Science
State University, Boulder, Colorado, June 1997
Minor: Statistics

An example of a format for a related courses section follows:

RELATED COURSES	
Database Administration	Urban Planning
Business Computer Applications	Economics
Business Research Design	Actuary Science

· ·

Experience

The experience section of your resume should be the most substantial part and should take up most of the space on the page. Employers want to see what kind of work history you have. They will look at your range of experiences, longevity in jobs, and specific tasks you are able to complete. This section may also be called "work experience," "related experience," "employment history," or "employment." No matter what you call this section, some important points to remember are the following:

1. **Describe your duties** as they relate to the position you are seeking.

2. **Emphasize major responsibilities** and indicate increases in responsibility. Include all relevant employment experiences: summer, part-time, internships, cooperative education, or self-employment.

3. **Emphasize skills,** especially those that transfer from one situation to another. The fact that you coordinated a student organization, chaired meetings, supervised others, and managed a budget leads one to suspect that you could coordinate other things as well.

4. **Use descriptive job titles** that provide information about what you did. A "Student Intern" should be more specifically stated as, for example, "Magazine Operations Intern." "Volunteer" is also too general; a title like "Peer Writing Tutor" would be more appropriate.

5. **Create word pictures** by using active verbs to start sentences. Describe *results* you have produced in the work you have done.

A limp description would say something like the following: "My duties included helping with production, proofreading, and editing. I used a word processing package to alter text." An action statement would be stated as follows: "Coordinated and assisted in the creative marketing of brochures and seminar promotions, becoming proficient in WordPerfect."

Remember, an accomplishment is simply a result, a final measurable product that people can relate to. A duty is not a result, it is an obligation—every job holder has duties. For an effective resume, list as many results as you can. To make the most of the limited space you have and to give your description impact, carefully select appropriate and accurate descriptors from the list of action words in Exhibit 2.2.

Exhibit 2.2

Resume Action Verbs

Achieved	Collected	Converted
Acted	Communicated	Coordinated
Administered	Compiled	Corrected
Advised	Completed	Created
Analyzed	Composed	Decreased
Assessed	Conceptualized	Defined
Assisted	Condensed	Demonstrated
Attained	Conducted	Designed
Balanced	Consolidated	Determined
Budgeted	Constructed	Developed
Calculated	Controlled	Directed

continued

continued

Documented	Learned	Received
Drafted	Lectured	Recommended
Edited	Led	Recorded
Eliminated	Maintained	Reduced
Ensured	Managed	Reinforced
Established	Mapped	Reported
Estimated	Marketed	Represented
Evaluated	Met	Researched
Examined	Modified	Resolved
Explained	Monitored	Reviewed
Facilitated	Negotiated	Scheduled
Finalized	Observed	Selected
Generated	Obtained	Served
Handled	Operated	Showed
Headed	Organized	Simplified
Helped	Participated	Sketched
Identified	Performed	Sold
Illustrated	Planned	Solved
Implemented	Predicted	Staffed
Improved	Prepared	Streamlined
Increased	Presented	Studied
Influenced	Processed	Submitted
Informed	Produced	Summarized
Initiated	Projected	Systematized
Innovated	Proposed	Tabulated
Instituted	Provided	Tested
Instructed	Qualified	Transacted
Integrated	Quantified	Updated
Interpreted	Questioned	Verified
Introduced	Realized	

Here are some traits that employers tell us they like to see:

❑ Teamwork

❑ Energy and motivation

❑ Learning and using new skills

❑ Demonstrated versatility

❑ Critical thinking

❑ Understanding how profits are created

❑ Displaying organizational acumen

- ❑ Communicating directly and clearly, in both writing and speaking
- ❑ Risk taking
- ❑ Willingness to admit mistakes
- ❑ Manifesting high personal standards

Solutions to Frequently Encountered Problems

Repetitive Employment with the Same Employer

EMPLOYMENT: **The Foot Locker,** Portland, Oregon. Summer 1991, 1992, 1993. Initially employed in high school as salesclerk. Due to successful performance, asked to return next two summers at higher pay with added responsibility. Ranked as the #2 salesperson the first summer and #1 the next two summers. Assisted in arranging eye-catching retail displays; served as manager of other summer workers during owner's absence.

A Large Number of Jobs

EMPLOYMENT: Recent Hospitality Industry Experience: Affiliated with four upscale hotel/restaurant complexes (September 1991–February 1994), where I worked part- and full-time as a waiter, bartender, disc jockey, and bookkeeper to produce income for college.

Several Positions with the Same Employer

EMPLOYMENT: Coca-Cola Bottling Co., Burlington, VT, 1991–94. In four years, I received three promotions, each with increased pay and responsibility.

Summer Sales Coordinator: Promoted to hire, train, and direct efforts of add-on staff of 15 college-age route salespeople hired to meet summer peak demand for product.

Sales Administrator: Promoted to run home office sales desk, managing accounts and associated delivery schedules for professional sales force of ten people. Intensive phone work, daily interaction with all personnel, and strong knowledge of product line required.

Route Salesperson: Summer employment to travel and tourism industry sites using Coke products. Met specific schedule demands, used good communication skills with wide variety of customers, and demonstrated strong selling skills. Named salesperson of the month for July and August of that year.

Questions Resume Writers Often Ask

How Far Back Should I Go in Terms of Listing Past Jobs?

Usually, listing three or four jobs should suffice. If you did something back in high school that has a bearing on your future aspirations for employment, by all means list the job. As you progress through your college career, high school jobs may be replaced on the resume by college employment.

Should I Differentiate between Paid and Nonpaid Employment?

Most employers are not initially as concerned about how much you were paid. They are anxious to know how much responsibility you held in your past employment. There is no need to specify that your work was volunteer if you had significant responsibilities.

How Should I Represent My Accomplishments or Work-Related Responsibilities?

Succinctly, but fully. In other words, give the employer enough information to arouse curiosity, but not so much detail that you leave nothing to the imagination. Besides, some jobs merit more lengthy explanations than others. Be sure to convey any information that can give an employer a better understanding of the depth of your involvement at work. Did you supervise others? How many? Did your efforts result in a more efficient operation? How much did you increase efficiency? Did you handle a budget? How much? Were you promoted in a short time? Did you work two jobs at once or 15 hours per week after high school? Where appropriate, quantify.

Should the Work Section Always Follow the Education Section on the Resume?

Always lead with your strengths. If your past work closely relates to the employment you now seek, put this section after the objective. Or, if you are weak on the academic side but have a surplus of good work experiences, consider reversing the order of your sections to lead with employment, followed by education.

How Should I Present My Activities, Honors, Awards, Professional Societies, and Affiliations?

This section of the resume can add valuable information for an employer to consider if used correctly. The rule of thumb for information in this section is to include only those activities that are in some way relevant to the objective stated on your resume. If you can draw a valid connection between your activities and your objective, include them; if not, leave them out.

Granted, this is hard to do. Center on the championship basketball team or coordinator of the biggest homecoming parade ever held are roles that have meaning for you and represent personal accomplishments you'd like to share. But the resume is a brief document, and the information you provide on it should help the employer make a decision about your job eligibility. Including personal details can be confusing and could hurt your candidacy. Limiting your activity list to a few very significant experiences can be very effective.

If you are applying for a position as a safety officer, your certificate in Red Cross lifesaving skills or CPR would be related and valuable. You would want to include it. If, however, you are applying for a job as a junior account executive in an advertising agency, that information would be unrelated and superfluous. Leave it out.

Professional affiliations and honors should *all* be listed; especially important are those related to your job objective. Social clubs and activities need not be a part of your resume unless you hold a significant office or you are looking for a position related to your membership. Be aware that most prospective employers' principle concerns are related to your employability, not your social life. If you have any, publications can be included as an addendum to your resume.

The focus of the resume is your experience and education. It is not necessary to describe your involvement in activities. However, if your resume needs to be lengthened, this section provides the freedom either to expand on or mention only briefly the contributions you have made. If you have made significant contributions (e.g., an officer of an organization or a particularly long tenure with a group), you may choose to describe them in more detail. It is not always necessary to include the dates of your memberships with your activities the way you would include job dates.

There are a number of different ways in which to present additional information. You may give this section a number of different titles. Assess what you want to list, and then use an appropriate title. Do not use extracurricular activities. This terminology is scholastic, not professional, and therefore not appropriate. The following are two examples:

❏ ACTIVITIES: Society for Technical Communication, Student Senate, Student Admissions Representative, Senior Class Officer

❏ ACTIVITIES: • Society for Technical Communication Member
• Student Senator
• Student Admissions Representative
• Senior Class Officer

The position you are looking for will determine what you should or should not include. *Always* look for a correlation between the activity and the prospective job.

How Should I Handle References?

The use of references is considered a part of the interview process, and they should never be listed on a resume. You would always provide references to a potential employer if requested to, so it is not even necessary to include this section on the resume if room does not permit. If space is available, it is acceptable to include one of the following statements:

- ❑ REFERENCES: Furnished upon request.

- ❑ REFERENCES: Available upon request.

Individuals used as references must be protected from unnecessary contacts. By including names on your resume, you leave your references unprotected. Overuse and abuse of your references will lead to less-than-supportive comments. Protect your references by giving out their names only when you are being considered seriously as a candidate for a given position.

THE FUNCTIONAL RESUME

The functional resume departs from a chronological resume in that it organizes information by specific accomplishments in various settings: previous jobs, volunteer work, associations, etc. This type of resume permits you to stress the substance of your experiences rather than the position titles you have held. (See Exhibit 2.3.) You should consider using a functional resume if you have held a series of similar jobs that relied on the same skills or abilities.

Exhibit 2.3

Functional Resume

RICHARD JOHNSON

Lawrence Hall, Room 234
University of Florida
Gainesville, FL 34233
(904) 555-2146

4020 Bay Road
Delray Beach, FL 33446
(561) 555-9943

OBJECTIVE

A position as a systems analyst for a major institution that will allow me to build upon my past experience and use my problem-solving skills.

continued

---

continued

CAPABILITIES

- Analytical problem solver
- Experienced systems analyst
- Experienced with library information systems
- Effective communicator
- Strong people skills

SELECTED ACCOMPLISHMENTS

SYSTEMS ANALYSIS: Through a college work-study program I achieved three years of progressively more challenging duties in the library at the University of Florida in Gainesville. I helped design and implement a new system for cataloging and retrieving periodicals and instructed library staff in its use. Worked with mainframe and PC hardware and a variety of software.

PROBLEM SOLVING: I worked in the university's admissions office, debugging a program to keep track of new student applications.

TEAM PLAYER: Collaborated with coworkers and professionals in other university departments including the registrar's office and two other libraries on campus.

AWARDS

Dean's List (7 semesters)

EMPLOYMENT HISTORY

Hayes Library, University of Florida, Gainesville, 1994–present
Admissions Office, University of Florida, Gainesville, 1993–1995

EDUCATION

Bachelor of Science
Computer Information Systems
University of Florida
Gainesville, Florida
June 1997

REFERENCES

Provided upon request.

The Objective

A functional resume begins with an objective that can be used to focus the contents of the resume.

Specific Accomplishments

Specific accomplishments are listed on this type of resume. Examples of the types of headings used to describe these capabilities might include sales, counseling, teaching, communication, production, management, marketing, or writing. The headings you choose will directly relate to your experience and the tasks that you carried out. Each accomplishment section contains statements related to your experience in that category, regardless of when or where it occurred. Organize the accomplishments and the related tasks you describe in their order of importance as related to the position you seek.

Experience or Employment History

Your actual work experience is condensed and placed after the specific accomplishments section. It simply lists dates of employment, position titles, and employer names.

Education

The education section of a functional resume is identical to that of the chronological resume, but it does not carry the same visual importance because it is placed near the bottom of the page.

References

Because actual reference names are never listed on a resume, this section is optional if space does not permit.

THE TARGETED RESUME

The targeted resume focuses on specific work-related capabilities you can bring to a given position within an organization. (See Exhibit 2.4.) It should be sent to an individual within the organization who makes hiring decisions about the position you are seeking.

The Objective

The objective on this type of resume should be targeted to a specific career or position. It should be supported by the capabilities, accomplishments, and achievements documented in the resume.

Exhibit 2.4

Targeted Resume

THOMAS R. BERNADINO

Lindsley Hall #450
University of Wisconsin
Madison, WI 53706
(608) 555-2478
(until June 1997)

878 Marion Street
Glenview, IL 60025
(847) 555-0980

JOB TARGET
CAD Specialist with an architectural design firm

CAPABILITIES
- Familiarity with a variety of CAD software
- Organizational skills
- Excellent communicator, both written and oral
- Proven team skills
- Bilingual, Spanish and English

ACHIEVEMENTS
- Several articles published in local newspapers
- Designed brochures and logos for campus student activity groups
- Worked on design of community Victory Garden project
- Maintained a 4.0 average throughout college

WORK HISTORY
1996–present Student Internship
Birch and Caplan Architectural Firm
Madison, WI
- Assisted several architects and draftsmen with a variety of projects including a new office building complex

1993–1996 Work-Study Position
Yearbook Office
University of Wisconsin, Madison, WI
- Using CAD software, designed the layout for three yearbooks

1993–1995 Summer Position (two summers)
Hahnaman Hospital, Chicago, IL
- Orderly for the pediatric unit. Performed a variety of duties following the directions of the nursing staff, including escorting patients to x-ray and the OR

continued

---

continued

EDUCATION
June 1997
Bachelor of Arts, Graphic Arts
University of Wisconsin, Madison, WI

Capabilities

Capabilities should be statements that illustrate tasks you believe you are capable of based on your accomplishments, achievements, and work history. Each should relate to your targeted career or position. You can stress your qualifications rather than your employment history. This approach may require research to obtain an understanding of the nature of the work involved and the capabilities necessary to carry out that work.

Accomplishments/Achievements

This section relates the various activities you have been involved in to the job market. These experiences may include previous jobs, extracurricular activities at school, internships, and part-time summer work.

Experience

Your work history should be listed in abbreviated form and may include position title, employer name, and employment dates.

Education

Because this type of resume is directed toward a specific job target and an individual's related experience, the education section is not prominently located at the top of the resume as is done on the chronological resume.

THE BROADCAST LETTER

The broadcast letter is used by some job seekers in place of a resume and cover letter. (See Exhibit 2.5.) The purpose of this type of document is to make a number of potential employers aware of the availability and expertise of the job seeker. Because the broadcast letter is mass-mailed (500–600 employers), the amount of work required may not be worth the return for many people. If you choose to mail out a broadcast letter, you can expect to receive a response from 2–5 percent, at best, of the organizations that receive your letter.

This type of document is most often used by individuals who have an extensive and quantifiable work history. College students often do not have the

Exhibit 2.5

Broadcast Letter

JAMAL ABUNAWARA
6324 Washington Avenue
Michigan Heights, Illinois 60615
(847) 555-3621

Ms. Susan Devons   June 6, 1997
Human Resources Director
Franklin HMO Group
5465 Lincoln Road
Chicago, IL 60646

Dear Ms. Devons,

I am writing to you because your corporation may be in need of a database administrator with a specialization in health care facilities. With my bachelor's degree from the University of Chicago and my four years of experience in a variety of health care settings, I have had the opportunity to work with a cross section of clients with a range of needs. I am able to adapt to different environments and put my skills and abilities to immediate use. Some highlights of my experience that might interest you include:

- During college I volunteered more than 400 hours in the finance department of my local hospital.

- After graduation I worked for three years with database management for a chain of top nursing homes, including restructuring the database, designing and installing a security system, and maintaining the efficiency of the database.

- I supervised a rotation of work-study students placed in my office.

I received my Bachelor or Science degree in Database Management in 1994 from the University of Chicago.

continued

continued

It would be a pleasure to review my qualifications with you in a personal interview at some mutually convenient time. I will call your office at the end of next week to make arrangements. I look forward to discussing career opportunities with Franklin HMO Group.

Sincerely,

Jamal Abunawara

credentials and work experience to support using a broadcast letter, and most will find it difficult to effectively quantify a slim work history.

A broadcast letter is generally five paragraphs (one page) long. The first paragraph should immediately gain the attention of the reader and state some unusual accomplishment or skill that would be of benefit to the organization. The second paragraph states the reason for the letter. Details of the sender's work history are revealed in the third paragraph. Education and other qualifications or credentials are then described. Finally, the job seeker indicates what he or she will do to follow up on the letter, which usually is a follow-up call 1–2 weeks after the letter is sent.

RESUME PRODUCTION AND OTHER TIPS

If you have the option and convenience of using a laser printer, you may want to initially produce a limited number of copies in case you want or need to make changes on your resume.

Resume paper color should be carefully chosen. You should consider the types of employers who will receive your resume and the types of positions for which you are applying. Use white or ivory paper for traditional or conservative employers, or for higher-level positions.

Black ink on sharply white paper can be harsh on the reader's eyes. Think about an ivory or cream paper that will provide less contrast and be easier to read. Pink, green, and blue tints should generally be avoided.

Many resume writers buy packages of matching envelopes and cover sheet stationery that, although not absolutely necessary, does convey a professional impression.

If you'll be producing many cover letters at home, be sure you have high-quality printing equipment, whether it be computerized or standard typewriter equipment. Learn standard envelope formats for business and retain a copy of every cover letter you send out. You can use it to take notes of any telephone conversations that may occur.

If attending a job fair, women generally can fold their resume in thirds lengthwise and find it fits into a clutch bag or envelope-style purse. Both men and women will have no trouble if they carry a briefcase. For men without a briefcase, carry the resume in a nicely covered legal-size pad holder or fold it in half lengthwise and place it inside your suitcoat pocket, taking care it doesn't "float" outside your collar.

THE COVER LETTER

The cover letter provides you with the opportunity to tailor your resume by telling the prospective employer how you can be a benefit to the organization. It will allow you to highlight aspects of your background that are not already discussed in your resume and that might be especially relevant to the organization you are contacting or to the position you are seeking. Every resume should have a cover letter enclosed when you send it out. Unlike the resume, which may be mass-produced, a cover letter is most effective when it is individually typed and focused on the particular requirements of the organization in question.

A good cover letter should supplement the resume and motivate the reader to review the resume. The format shown in Exhibit 2.6 is only a suggestion to help you decide what information to include in writing a cover letter.

Begin the cover letter with your street address 12 lines down from the top. Leave three to five lines between the date and the name of the person to whom

---

Exhibit 2.6

Cover Letter Format

Your Street Address
Your Town, State, Zip
Phone Number
Date

continued

continued

Name
Title
Organization
Address

Dear _____ :

First Paragraph. In this paragraph, state the reason for the letter, name the specific position or type of work you are applying for, and indicate from which resource (career development office, newspaper, contact, employment service) you learned of the opening. The first paragraph can also be used to inquire about future openings.

Second Paragraph. Indicate why you are interested in the position, the company, its products or services, and what you can do for the employer. If you are a recent graduate, explain how your academic background makes you a qualified candidate. Try not to repeat the same information found in the resume.

Third Paragraph. Refer the reader to the enclosed resume for more detailed information.

Fourth Paragraph. In this paragraph, say what you will do to follow up on your letter. For example, state that you will call by a certain date to set up an interview or to find out if the company will be recruiting in your area. Finish by indicating your willingness to answer any questions they may have. Be sure you have provided your phone number.

Sincerely,

Type your name

Enclosure

you are addressing the cover letter. Make sure you leave one blank line between the salutation and the body of the letter and between each paragraph.

After typing "Sincerely," leave four blank lines and type your name. This should leave plenty of room for your signature. A sample cover letter is shown in Exhibit 2.7.

The following are guidelines that will help you write good cover letters:

1. Be sure to type your letter; ensure there are no misspellings.

Exhibit 2.7

Sample Cover Letter

JUDITH LEVINSON
435 Winchester Street
Brookline, MA 02146
(617) 555-4434

April 25, 1997

John Sullivan
Director of Personnel
Colonial Williamsburg Foundation
P.O. Drawer T
Williamsburg, VA 23185

Dear Mr. Sullivan,

In May of 1997 I will graduate from Tufts University with a Bachelor of Science degree in computer programming. I read of your opening for a researcher conversant with Internet search engines in *The Herald* on Sunday, April 24, 1997, and I am very interested in the possibilities it offers. I am writing to explore the opportunity for employment with the Foundation.

The ad indicated you were looking for creative individuals with an interest in U.S. history and good research and communication skills. I believe I possess those qualities. During the summers while in college I worked at Plimoth Plantation in several capacities, including character interpreter and as an assistant in the research department. Through my work there, I learned the importance of possessing good organizational skills and maintaining a positive attitude with coworkers and visitors.

In addition to the various computer courses in my academic program, I felt it important to enroll in some history, anthropology,

continued

continued

and psychology courses, focusing particularly on research design and methods. These courses helped me become comfortable with understanding eighteenth-century American culture, as well as honing my research skills. These accomplishments I believe will help me to represent the Colonial Williamsburg Foundation in a professional and enthusiastic manner.

I would like to meet with you to discuss how my education and experience would be consistent with your needs. I will contact your office next week to discuss the possibility of an interview. In the meantime, if you have any questions or require additional information, please contact me at my home, (617) 555-4434, or via e-mail at JudLevin@theonramp.net.

Sincerely,

Judith Levinson

Enclosure

2. Avoid unusual typefaces, such as script.

3. Address the letter to an individual, using the person's name and title. To obtain this information, call the company. If answering a blind newspaper advertisement, address the letter "To Whom It May Concern" or omit the salutation.

4. Be sure your cover letter directly indicates the position you are applying for and tells why you are qualified to fill it.

5. Send the original letter, not a photocopy, with your resume. Keep a copy for your records.

6. Make your cover letter no more than one page.

7. Include a phone number where you can be reached.

8. Avoid trite language and have someone read it over to react to its tone, content, and mechanics.

9. For your own information, record the date you send out each letter and resume.

CHAPTER THREE

RESEARCHING CAREERS

....

One common question a career counselor is asked is "What can I do with my degree?" Computer majors might know the type of computer work they want to do—programming, systems analysis, database administration, software or hardware design, or even sales and service—but they could be unsure of the various job settings in which work is available. These days, almost every type of service, industry, or institution depends on the services of some sort of computer professional. But would you fit in more comfortably at a large corporation, or a small private business; working with the government; for a hospital or an educational institution; or any other number of settings? The choices really are limitless.

....

What Do They Call the Job You Want?

There is every reason to be unaware. One reason for confusion is perhaps a mistaken assumption that a college education provides job training. In most cases, it does not. Of course, applied fields such as engineering, management, and computer science provide specific skills for the workplace, but the more broad-based your program is the less this will be true. A liberal arts education exposes you to numerous fields of study and teaches you quantitative reasoning, critical thinking, writing, and speaking, all of which can be successfully applied to a number of different job fields. Even for someone majoring in an applied field, a more broad-based education can sometimes prove to be an advantage in the long run.

As indicated in Chapter 1 on self-assessment, your first task is to understand and value what parts of that education you enjoyed and were good at and would continue to enjoy in your life's work. Did your writing courses encourage you in your ability to express yourself in writing? Did you enjoy the research process and did you find your work was well received? Did you enjoy any of your required quantitative subjects like algebra or calculus?

The answers to questions such as these provide clues to skills and interests you bring to the employment market over and above the credential of your degree. In fact, it is not an overstatement to suggest that most employers who demand a college degree immediately look beyond that degree to you as a person and your own individual expression of what you like to do and think you can do for them, regardless of your major.

Collecting Job Titles

The world of employment is a big place, and even seasoned veterans of the job hunt can be surprised about what jobs are to be found in what organizations. You need to become a bit of an explorer and adventurer and be willing to try a variety of techniques to begin a list of possible occupations that might use your talents and education. Once you have a list of possibilities that you are interested in and qualified for, you can move on to find out what kinds of organizations have these job titles.

....

Not every employer seeking to hire someone with a computer degree may be equally desirable to you. Some employment environments may be more attractive to you than others. A computer programmer wanting to work with business systems could do that for a large corporation, for a small firm within a corporation, for a private concern, for the government, a financial institution, or even in a hospital setting. Each of these environments presents a different "culture" with associated norms in the pace of work, the subject matter of interest, and the backgrounds of its employees. Although the job titles may be the same, not all locations may present the same "fit" for you.

If you majored in computer science and enjoyed the exacting, detailed work you did as part of your degree and have developed some strong investigative skills, you might naturally think about systems analysis or computer engineering. But computer science majors with these same skills and interests might go on to teach others their skills, or work as software engineers or CAD specialists. Each of these job titles can also be found in a number of different settings.

....

Take training, for example. Trainers write policy and procedural manuals and actively teach to assist all levels of employees in mastering various tasks and work-related systems. Trainers exist in all large corporations, banks, consumer goods manufacturers, medical diagnostic equipment firms, sales organizations, and any organization that has processes or materials that need to be presented to and learned by the staff.

In reading job descriptions or want ads for any of these positions, you would find your four-year degree a "must." However, the academic major might be less important than your own individual skills in critical thinking, analysis, report writing, public presentations, and interpersonal communication. Even more important than thinking or knowing you have certain skills is your ability to express those skills concretely and the examples you use to illustrate them to an employer.

The best beginning to a job search is to create a list of job titles you might want to pursue, learn more about the nature of the jobs behind those titles, and then discover what kinds of employers hire for those positions. In the following section, we'll teach you how to build a job title directory to use in your job search.

Developing a Job Title Directory That Works for You

A job title directory is simply a complete list of all the job titles you are interested in, are intrigued by, or think you are qualified for. Combining the understanding gained through self-assessment with your own individual interests and the skills and talents you've acquired with your degree, you'll soon start to read and recognize a number of occupational titles that seem right for you. There are several resources you can use to develop your list, including computer searches, books, and want ads.

Computerized Interest Inventories. One way to begin your search is to identify a number of jobs that call for your degree and the particular skills and interests you identified as part of the self-assessment process. There are on the market excellent interactive computer career guidance programs to help you produce such selected lists of possible job titles. Most of these are available at high schools and colleges and at some larger town and city libraries. Two of the industry leaders are SIGI and DISCOVER. Both allow you to enter interests, values, educational background, and other information to produce lists of possible occupations and industries. Each of the resources listed here will produce different job title lists. Some job titles will appear again and again, while others will be unique to a particular source. Investigate them all!

Reference Books.   Books on the market that may be available through your local library, bookstore, or career counseling office also suggest various occupations related to a number of majors. The following are only two of the many good books on the market: *Occupational Outlook Handbook* and *Occupational Projections and Training Data,* both put out annually by the U.S. Department of Labor, Bureau of Labor Statistics. The *OOH* describes hundreds of job titles under several broad categories such as Executive, Administrative, and Managerial Occupations and also identifies those jobs by their *Dictionary of Occupational Titles* DOT code. (See following discussion.)

....

> For computer majors more than two dozen related job titles are listed throughout various sections of the *OOH.* Some are familiar ones such as computer programmer or computer engineer, and others are interestingly different, such as database administrator or computer support analyst.
>
> The *Occupational Projections and Training Data* is another good resource that allows job seekers to compare 500 occupations on factors such as job openings, earnings, and training requirements.
>
> If, for example, you discover systems analyst as a job title in the *OOH,* you can then go to the *Occupational Projections and Training Data* and find scores of jobs related to that title. This source adds some depth by presenting statistics in a number of different occupations within that field.

....

Each job title deserves your consideration. Like the layers of an onion, the search for job titles can go on and on! As you spend time doing this activity, you are actually learning more about the value of your degree. What's important in your search at this point is not to become critical or selective, but rather to develop as long a list of possibilities as you can. Every source used will help you add new and potentially exciting jobs to your growing list.

Want Ads.   It has been well publicized that newspaper want ads represent only about 10–15 percent of the current job market. Nevertheless, the Sunday want ads can be a great help to you in your search. Although they may not be the best place to look for a job, they can teach the job seeker much about the job market and provide a good education in job descriptions, duties and responsibilities, active industries, and some indication of the volume of job traffic. For our purposes, they are a good source for job titles to add to your list.

Read the Sunday want ads in a major market newspaper for several Sundays in a row. Circle and then cut out any and all ads that interest you and seem to call for something close to your education and experience. Remember, because want ads are written for what an organization *hopes* to find, you don't have to meet absolutely every criterion. However, if certain requirements are stated as absolute minimums and you cannot meet them, it's best not to waste your time.

A recent examination of *The Boston Sunday Globe* reveals the following possible occupations for a liberal arts major with some computer skills and limited prior work experience. (This is only a partial list of what was available.)

- Admissions representative
- Technical writer
- Salesperson
- Personnel trainee
- Compliance director
- GED examiner
- Assistant principal gifts writer
- Direct mail researcher
- Public relations officer
- Associate publicist

After performing this exercise for a few Sundays, you'll find you have collected a new library of job titles.

The Sunday want ad exercise is important because these jobs are out in the marketplace. They truly exist, and people with your qualifications are being sought to apply. What's more, many of these advertisements describe the duties and responsibilities of the job advertised and give you a beginning sense of the challenges and opportunities such a position presents. Some will indicate salary, and that will be helpful as well. This information will better define the jobs for you and provide some good material for possible interviews in that field.

Exploring Job Descriptions

Once you've arrived at a solid list of possible job titles that interest you and for which you believe you are somewhat qualified, it's a good idea to do some research on each of these jobs. The preeminent source for such job information is the *Dictionary of Occupational Titles,* or DOT. This directory lists every conceivable job and provides excellent up-to-date information on duties and responsibilities, interactions with associates, and day-to-day assignments and tasks. These descriptions provide a thorough job analysis, but they do not consider the possible employers or the environments in which this job may be performed. So, although a position as public relations officer may be well defined in terms of duties and responsibilities, it does not explain the differences in doing public relations work in a college or a hospital or a factory or a bank. You will need to look somewhere else for work settings.

Learning More about Possible Work Settings

After reading some job descriptions, you may choose to edit and revise your list of job titles once again, discarding those you feel are not suitable and keeping those that continue to hold your interest. Or you may wish to keep your list intact and see where these jobs may be located. For example, if you are interested in public relations and you appear to have those skills and the requisite education, you'll want to know what organizations do public relations. How can you find that out? How much income does someone in public relations make a year and what is the employment potential for the field of public relations?

To answer these and many other good questions about your list of job titles, we will direct you to any of the following resources: *Careers Encyclopedia, Career Information Center, College to Career: The Guide to Job Opportunities,* and the *Occupational Outlook Handbook.* Each of these books, in a different way, will help to put the job titles you have selected into an employer context. *VGM'S Handbook for Business and Management Careers* shows detailed career descriptions for over 50 fields. Entries include complete information on duties and responsibilities for individual careers and detailed entry-level requirements. There is information on working conditions and promotional opportunities as well. Salary ranges and career outlook projections are also provided. Perhaps the most extensive discussion is found in the *Occupational Outlook Handbook,* which gives a thorough presentation of the nature of the work, the working conditions, employment statistics, training, other qualifications, and advancement possibilities as well as job outlook and earnings. Related occupations are also detailed, and a select bibliography is provided to help you find additional information.

Continuing with our public relations example, your search through these reference materials would teach you that the public relations jobs you find attractive are available in larger hospitals, financial institutions, most corporations (both consumer goods and industrial goods), media organizations, and colleges and universities.

Networking to Get the Complete Story

You now have not only a list of job titles but also, for each of these job titles, a description of the work involved and a general list of possible employment settings in which to work. You'll want to do some reading and keep talking to friends, colleagues, teachers, and others about the possibilities. Don't neglect to ask if the career office at your college maintains some kind of alumni network. Often such alumni networks will connect you with another graduate from the college who is working in the job title or industry you are seeking information about. These career networkers offer what assistance they can. For some, it is a full day "shadowing" the alumnus as he or she goes about the job. Others offer partial day visits, tours, informational interviews, resume reviews, job postings, or, if distance prevents a visit, telephone interviews. As fellow graduates, they'll be frank and informative about their own jobs and prospects in their field.

Take them up on their offer and continue to learn all you can about your own personal list of job titles, descriptions, and employment settings. You'll probably continue to edit and refine this list as you learn more about the realities of the job, the possible salary, advancement opportunities, and supply and demand statistics.

In the next section, we'll describe how to find the specific organizations that represent these industries and employers, so that you can begin to make contact.

WHERE ARE THESE JOBS, ANYWAY?

Having a list of job titles that you've designed around your own career interests and skills is an excellent beginning. It means you've really thought about who you are and what you are presenting to the employment market. It has caused you to think seriously about the most appealing environments to work in, and you have identified some employer types that represent these environments.

The research and the thinking that you've done this far will be used again and again. It will be helpful in writing your resume and cover letters, in talking about yourself on the telephone to prospective employers, and in answering interview questions.

Now is a good time to begin to narrow the field of job titles and employment sites down to some specific employers to initiate the employment contact.

Finding Out Which Employers Hire People Like You

This section will provide tips, techniques, and specific resources for developing an actual list of specific employers that can be used to make contacts. It is only an outline that you must be prepared to tailor to your own particular needs and according to what you bring to the job search. Once again, it is important to stress the need to communicate with others along the way exactly what you're looking for and what your goals are for the research you're doing. Librarians, employers, career counselors, friends, friends of friends, business contacts, and bookstore staff will all have helpful information on geographically specific and new resources to aid you in locating employers who'll hire you.

Identifying Information Resources

Your interview wardrobe and your new resume may have put a dent in your wallet, but the resources you'll need to pursue your job search are available for free (although you might choose to copy materials on a machine instead of taking notes by hand). The categories of information detailed here are not hard to find and are yours for the browsing.

Numerous resources described in this section will help you identify actual employers. Use all of them or any others that you identify as available in your geographic area. As you become experienced in this process, you'll quickly figure out which information sources are helpful and which are not. If you live in a rural area, a well-planned day trip to a major city that includes a college career office, a large college or city library, state and federal employment centers, a chamber of commerce office, and a well-stocked bookstore can produce valuable results.

There are many excellent resources available to help you identify actual job sites. They are categorized into employer directories (usually indexed by product lines and geographic location), geographically based directories (designed to highlight particular cities, regions, or states), career-specific directories (e.g., *Sports Market Place,* which lists tens of thousands of firms involved with sports), periodicals and newspapers, targeted job posting publications, and videos. This is by no means meant to be a complete list of resources, but rather a starting point for identifying useful resources.

Working from the more general references to highly specific resources, we will provide a basic list to help you begin your search. Many of these you'll find easily available. In some cases, reference librarians and others will suggest even better materials for your particular situation. Start to create your own customized bibliography of job search references. Use copying services to save time and to allow you to carry away information about organization mission, location, company officers, phone numbers, and addresses.

Employer Directories. There are many employer directories available to give you the kind of information you need for your job search. Some of our favorites are listed here, but be sure to ask the professionals you are working with to make additional suggestions.

❑ *America's Corporate Families* identifies many major U.S. ultimate parent companies and displays corporate family linkage of subsidiaries and divisions. Businesses can be identified by their industrial code.

❑ *Million Dollar Directory: America's Leading Public and Private Companies* lists about 160,000 companies.

❑ *Moody's* various manuals are intended as guides for investors, so they contain a history of each company. Each manual contains a classification of companies by industries and products.

❏ *Standard and Poor's Register of Corporations* contains listings for 45,000 businesses, some of which are not listed in the *Million Dollar Directory*.

❏ *Job Seeker's Guide to Private and Public Companies* profiles 15,000 employers in four volumes, each covering a different geographic region. Company entries include contact information, business descriptions, and application procedures.

❏ *The Career Guide: Dun's Employment Opportunities Directory* includes more than 5,000 large organizations, including hospitals and local governments. Profiles include an overview and history of the employer as well as opportunities, benefits, and contact names. It contains geographic and industrial indexes and indexes by discipline or internship availability. This guide also includes a state-by-state list of professional personnel consultants and their specialties.

❏ *Professional's Job Finder/Government Job Finder/Non-Profits Job Finder* are specific directories of job services, salary surveys, and periodical listings in which to find advertisements for jobs in the professional, government, or not-for-profit sector.

❏ *Opportunities in Nonprofit Organizations* is a VGM career series edition that opens up the world of not-for-profit by helping you match your interest profile to the aims and objectives of scores of nonprofit employers in business, education, health and medicine, social welfare, science and technology, and many others. There is also a special section on fundraising and development career paths.

❏ *The 100 Best Companies to Sell For* lists companies by industry and provides contact information and describes benefits and corporate culture.

❏ *The 100 Best Companies to Work For in America* rates organizations on several factors including opportunities, job security, and pay.

❏ *Companies That Care* lists organizations that the authors believe are family-friendly. One index organizes information by state.

❏ *Infotrac CD-ROM Business Index* covers business journals and magazines as well as news magazines and can provide information on public and private companies.

❏ *ABI/INFORM On Disc* (CD-ROM) indexes articles in over 800 journals.

Geographically Based Directories.   The Job Bank series published by Bob Adams, Inc. contains detailed entries on each area's major employers, including business activity, address, phone number, and hiring contact name. Many listings specify educational backgrounds being sought in potential employees. Each volume contains a solid discussion of each city's or state's major employment sectors. Organizations are also indexed by industry. Job Bank volumes are available for the following places: Atlanta, Boston, Chicago, Denver, Dallas–Ft. Worth, Florida, Houston, Ohio, St. Louis, San Francisco, Seattle, Los Angeles, New York, Detroit, Philadelphia, Minneapolis, the Northwest, and Washington, D.C.

National Job Bank lists employers in every state, along with contact names and commonly hired job categories. Included are many small companies often overlooked by other directories. Companies are also indexed by industry. This publication provides information on educational backgrounds sought and lists company benefits.

Career-Specific Directories. VGM publishes a number of excellent series detailing careers for college graduates. In the *Professional Career Series* are guides to careers in the following fields, among others:

❑ Advertising

❑ Communications

❑ Business

❑ Computers

❑ Health Care

❑ High Tech

Each provides an excellent discussion of the industry, educational requirements for jobs, salary ranges, duties, and projected outlooks for the field.

Another VGM series, *Opportunities In . . .,* has an equally wide range of titles relating to your major, such as the following:

❑ *Opportunities in Banking*

❑ *Opportunities in Insurance*

❑ *Opportunities in Sports and Athletics*

❑ *Opportunities in Journalism*

❑ *Opportunities in Marketing*

❑ *Opportunities in Television and Radio*

Sports Market Place (Sportsguide) lists organizations by sport. It also describes trade/professional associations, college athletic organizations, multi-sport publications, media contacts, corporate sports sponsors, promotion/event/athletic management services, and trade shows.

Periodicals and Newspapers. Several sources are available to help you locate which journals or magazines carry job advertisements in your field. Other resources help you identify opportunities in other parts of the country.

❑ *Where the Jobs Are: A Comprehensive Directory of 1200 Journals Listing Career Opportunities* links specific occupational titles to corresponding periodicals that carry job listings for your field.

❑ *Social & Behavioral Sciences Jobs Handbook* contains a periodicals matrix organized by academic discipline and highlights periodicals containing job listings.

❑ *National Business Employment Weekly* compiles want ads from four regional editions of the *Wall Street Journal.* Most are business and management positions.

❑ *National Ad Search* reprints ads from 75 metropolitan newspapers across the country. Although the focus is on management positions, technical and professional postings are also included. *Caution:* Watch deadline dates carefully on listings, because deadlines may have already passed by the time the ad is printed.

❑ *The Federal Jobs Digest* and *Federal Career Opportunities* list government positions.

❑ *World Chamber of Commerce Directory* lists addresses for chambers worldwide, state boards of tourism, convention and visitors' bureaus, and economic development organizations.

This list is certainly not exhaustive; use it to begin your job search work.

Targeted Job Posting Publications. Although the resources that follow are national in scope, they are either targeted to one medium of contact (telephone), focused on specific types of jobs, or are less comprehensive than the sources previously listed.

❑ *Job Hotlines USA* pinpoints over 1,000 hard-to-find telephone numbers for companies and government agencies that use prerecorded job messages and listings. Very few of the telephone numbers listed are toll-free, and sometimes recordings are long, so callers beware!

❑ *The Job Hunter* is a national biweekly newspaper listing business, arts, media, government, human services, health, community-related, and student services job openings.

❑ *Current Jobs for Graduates* is a national employment listing for liberal arts professions, including editorial positions, management opportunities, museum work, teaching, and nonprofit work.

❑ *Environmental Opportunities* serves environmental job interests nationwide by listing administrative, marketing, and human resources positions along with education-related jobs and positions directly related to a degree in an environmental field.

❑ *Y National Vacancy List* shows YMCA professional vacancies, including development, administration, programming, membership, and recreation postings.

❑ *ARTSearch* is a national employment service bulletin for the arts, including administration, managerial, marketing, and financial management jobs.

❑ *Community Jobs* is an employment newspaper for the nonprofit sector that provides a variety of listings, including project manager, canvas director, government relations specialist, community organizer, and program instructor.

❑ *College Placement Council Annual: A Guide to Employment Opportunities for College Graduates* is an annual guide containing solid job-hunting information and, more importantly, displaying ads from large corporations actively seeking recent college graduates in all majors. Company profiles provide brief descriptions and available employment opportunities. Contact names and addresses are given. Profiles are indexed by organization name, geographic location, and occupation.

Videos.   You may be one of the many job seekers who like to get information via a medium other than paper. Many career libraries, public libraries, and career centers in libraries carry an assortment of videos that will help you learn new techniques and get information helpful in the job search. A small sampling of the multitude of videos now available includes the following:

❑ *The Skills Search* (20 min.) discusses three types of skills important in the workplace, how to present the skills in an interview, and how to respond to problem questions.

❑ *Effective Answers to Interview Questions* (35 min.) presents two real-life job seekers and shows how they realized the true meaning of interview questions and formulated positive answers.

❑ *Employer's Expectations* (33 min.) covers three areas that are important to all employers: appearance, dependability, and skills.

❏ *The Tough New Labor Market of the 1990s* (30 min.) presents labor market facts as well as suggestions on what job seekers should do to gain employment in this market.

❏ *Dialing for Jobs: Using the Phone in the Job Search* (30 min.) describes how to use the phone effectively to gain information and arrange interviews by following two new graduates as they learn and apply techniques.

Locating Information Resources

An essay by John Case that appeared in the *Boston Globe* (August 25, 1993) alerts both new and seasoned job seekers that the job market is changing, and the old guarantees of lifelong employment no longer hold true. Some of our major corporations, which were once seen as the most prestigious of employment destinations, are now laying off thousands of employees. Middle management is especially hard hit in downsizing situations. On the other side of the coin, smaller, more entrepreneurial firms are adding employees and realizing enormous profit margins. The geography of the new job market is unfamiliar, and the terrain is much harder to map. New and smaller firms can mean different kinds of jobs and new job titles. The successful job seeker will keep an open mind about where he or she might find employment and what that employment might be called.

In order to become familiar with this new terrain, you will need to undertake some research, which can be done at any of the following locations:

❏ Public libraries

❏ Business organizations

❏ Employment agencies

❏ Bookstores

❏ Career libraries

Each one of these places offers a collection of resources that will help you get the information you need.

As you meet and talk with service professionals at all these sites, be sure to let them know what you're doing. Inform them of your job search, what you've already accomplished, and what you're looking for. The more people who know you're job seeking, the greater the possibility that someone will have information or know someone who can help you along your way.

Public Libraries.   Large city libraries, college and university libraries, and even well-supported town library collections contain a variety of resources to help you conduct a job search. It is not uncommon for libraries to have separate "vocational choices" sections with books, tapes, and associated materials relating to job search and selection. Some are now even making resume creation software available for use by patrons.

Some of the publications we name throughout this book are expensive reference items that are rarely purchased by individuals. In addition, libraries carry a wide range of newspapers and telephone yellow pages as well as the usual array of books. If resources are not immediately available, many libraries have loan arrangements with other facilities and can make information available to you relatively quickly.

Take advantage of not only the reference collections, but also the skilled and informed staff. Let them know exactly what you are looking for, and they'll have their own suggestions. You'll be visiting the library frequently, and the reference staff will soon come to know who you are and what you're working on. They'll be part of your job search network!

Business Organizations. Chambers of Commerce, Offices of New Business Development, Councils on Business and Industry, Small Business Administration (SBA) offices, and professional associations can all provide geographically specific lists of companies and organizations that have hiring needs. They also have an array of other available materials, including visitors' guides and regional fact books that provide additional employment information.

These agencies serve to promote local and regional businesses and ensure their survival and success. Although these business organizations do not advertise job openings or seek employees for their members, they may be very aware of staffing needs among their member firms. In your visits to each of these locations, spend some time with the personnel getting to know who they are and what they do. Let them know of your job search and your intentions regarding employment. You may be surprised and delighted at the information they may provide.

Employment Agencies. Employment agencies, including state and federal employment offices, professional "head hunters" or executive search firms, and some private career counselors can provide direct leads to job openings. Don't overlook these resources. If you are mounting a complete job search program and want to ensure that you are covering the potential market for employers, consider the employment agencies in your territory. Some of these organizations work contractually with several specific firms and may have access that is unavailable to you. Others may be particularly well-informed about supply and demand in particular industries or geographic locations.

In the case of professional (commercial) employment agencies, which include those executive recruitment firms labeled "head hunters," you should be cautious about entering into any binding contractual agreement. Before doing so, be sure to get the information you need to decide whether their services can be of use to you. Questions to ask include the following: Who pays the fee when employment is obtained? Are there any other fees or costs associated with this service? What is their placement rate? Can you see a list of previous clients and can you talk to any for references? Do they typically work with entry-level job seekers? Do they tend to focus on particular kinds of employment or industries?

A few cautions are in order, however, when you work with professional agencies. Remember, the professional employment agency is, in most cases, paid by the hiring organization. Naturally, their interest and attention is largely directed to the employer, not to the candidate. Of course, they want to provide good candidates to guarantee future contracts, but they are less interested in the job seeker than the employer.

For teacher candidates, there are a number of good placement firms that charge the prospective teacher, not the employer. This situation has evolved over time as a result of supply and demand and financial structuring of most school systems, which cannot spend money on recruiting teachers. Usually these firms charge a nonrefundable administrative fee and, upon successful placement, require a fee based on percentage of salary, which may range from 10–20 percent of annual compensation. Often, this can be repaid over a number of months. Check your contract carefully.

State and federal employment offices are no-fee services that maintain extensive "job boards" and can provide detailed specifications for each job advertised and help with application forms. Because government employment application forms are detailed, keep a master copy along with copies of all additional documentation (resumes, educational transcripts, military discharge papers, proof of citizenship, etc.). Successive applications may require separate filings. Visit these offices as frequently as you can, because most deal with applicants on a "walk-in" basis and will not telephone prospective candidates or maintain files of job seekers. Check your telephone book for the address of the nearest state and federal offices.

One type of employment service that causes much confusion among job seekers is the outplacement firm. Their advertisements tend to suggest they will put you in touch with the "hidden job market." They use advertising phrases such as "We'll work with you until you get that job," or "Maximize your earnings and career opportunities." In fact, if you read the fine print on these ads, you will notice these firms must state they are "Not an employment agency." These firms are, in fact, corporate and private outplacement counseling agencies whose work involves resume editing, counseling to provide leads for jobs, interview skills training, and all the other aspects of hiring preparation. They do this for a fee, sometimes in the thousands of dollars, which is paid by you, the client. Some of these firms have good reputations and provide excellent materials and techniques. Most, however, provide a service you as a college student or graduate can receive free from your alma mater or through a reciprocity agreement between your college and a college or university located closer to your current address.

Bookstores. Any well-stocked bookstore will carry some job search books that are worth buying. Some major stores will even have an extensive section devoted to materials, including excellent videos, related to the job search process. Several possibilities are listed in following sections. You will also find copies of local newspapers and business magazines. The one advantage that is provided by resources purchased at a bookstore is that you can read and work with the information in the comfort of your own home and do not have to conform to the hours of operation of a library, which can present real difficulties if you are working full time as you seek employment. A few minutes spent browsing in a bookstore might be a beneficial break from your job search activities and turn up valuable resources.

Career Libraries. Career libraries, which are found in career centers at colleges and universities and sometimes within large public libraries, contain a unique blend of the job search resources housed in other settings. In addition, career libraries often purchase a number of job listing publications, each of which targets a specific industry or type of job. You may find job listings specifically for entry-level positions for computer science majors. Ask about job posting newsletters or newspapers specifically focused on careers in the area that most interests you. Each center will be unique, but you are certain to discover some good sources of jobs.

Most college career libraries now hold growing collections of video material on specific industries and on aspects of your job search process, including dress and appearance, how to manage the luncheon or dinner interview, how to be effective at a job fair, and many other specific titles. Some larger corporations produce handsome video materials detailing the variety of career paths and opportunities available in their organizations.

Some career libraries also house computer-based career planning and information systems. These interactive computer programs help you to clarify your values and interests and will combine that with your education to provide possible job titles and industry locations. Some even contain extensive lists of graduate school programs.

One specific kind of service a career library will be able to direct you to is computerized job search services. These services, of which there are many, are run by private companies, individual colleges, or consortiums of colleges. They attempt to match qualified job candidates with potential employers. The candidate submits a resume (or an application) to the service. This information (which can be categorized into hundreds of separate "fields" of data) is entered into a computer database. Your information is then compared with the information from employers about what they desire in a prospective employee. If there is a "match" between what they want and what you have indicated you can offer, the job search service or the employer will contact you directly to continue the process.

Computerized job search services can complement an otherwise complete job search program. They are *not*, however, a substitute for the kinds of activities described in this book. They are essentially passive operations that are random in nature. If you have not listed skills, abilities, traits, experiences, or education *exactly* as an employer has listed its needs, there is simply no match.

Consult with the staff members at the career libraries you use. These professionals have been specifically trained to meet the unique needs you present. Often you can just drop in and receive help with general questions, or you may want to set up an appointment to speak one-on-one with a career counselor to gain special assistance.

Every career library is different in size and content, but each can provide valuable information for the job search. Some may even provide some limited counseling. If you have not visited the career library at your college or alma mater, call and ask if these collections are still available for your use. Be sure to ask about other services that you can use as well.

If you are not near your own college as you work on your job search, call the career office and inquire about reciprocal agreements with other colleges that are closer to where you live. Very often, your own alma mater can arrange for you to use a limited menu of services at another school. This typically would include access to a career library and job posting information and might include limited counseling.

CHAPTER FOUR

NETWORKING

etworking is the process of deliberately establishing relationships to get career-related information or to alert potential employers that you are available for work. Networking is critically important to today's job seeker for two reasons: it will help you get the information you need, and it can help you find out about *all* of the available jobs.

Getting the Information You Need

Networkers will review your resume and give you candid feedback on its effectiveness. They will talk about the job you are looking for and give you a candid appraisal of how they see your strengths and weaknesses. If they have a good sense of the industry or the employment sector for that job, you'll get their feelings on future trends in the industry as well. Some networkers will be very candid about salaries, job hunting techniques, and suggestions for your job search strategy. Many have been known to place calls right from the interview desk to friends and associates that might be interested in you. Each networker will make his or her own contribution, and each will be valuable.

Because organizations must evolve to adapt to current global market needs, the information provided by decision makers within various organizations will be critical to your success as a new job market entrant. For example, you might learn about the concept of virtual organizations from a networker. Virtual organizations are those that are temporarily established to take advantage of fast-changing opportunities and then dissolved. This concept is being discussed and implemented by chief executive officers of many organizations, including Corning, Apple, and Digital. Networking can help you find out about this and other trends currently affecting the industries under your consideration.

Finding Out about All of the Available Jobs

Secondly, not every job that is available at this very moment is advertised for potential applicants to see. This is called the *hidden job market*. Only 15–20 percent of all jobs are formally advertised, which means that 80–85 percent of available jobs do not appear in published channels. Networking will help you become more knowledgeable about all the employment opportunities available during your job search period.

Although someone you might talk to today doesn't know of any openings within his or her organization, tomorrow or next week or next month an opening may occur. If you've taken the time to show an interest in and knowledge of their organization, if you've shown the company representative how you can help achieve organizational goals and that you can fit into the organization, you'll be one of the first candidates considered for the position.

Networking: A Proactive Approach

Networking is a proactive rather than a reactive approach. You, as a job seeker, are expected to initiate a certain level of activity on your own behalf; you cannot afford to simply respond to jobs listed in the newspaper. Being proactive means building a network of contacts that includes informed and interested decision makers who will provide you with up-to-date knowledge of the current job market and increase your chances of finding out about employment opportunities appropriate for your interests, experience, and level of education.

An old axiom of networking says, "You are only two phone calls away from the information you need." In other words, by talking to enough people, you will quickly come across someone who can offer you help. Start with your professors. Each of them probably has a wide circle of contacts. In their work and travel they might have met someone who can help you or direct you to someone who can.

Control and the Networking Process

In deliberately establishing relationships, the process of networking begins with you in control—*you* are contacting specific individuals. As your network expands and you establish a set of professional relationships, your search for information or jobs will begin to move outside of your total control. A part of the networking process involves others assisting you by gathering information for you or recommending you as a possible job candidate. As additional people become a part of your networking system, you will have less knowledge about activities undertaken on your behalf; you will undoubtedly be contacted by individuals whom you did not initially approach. If you want to function effectively in surprise situations, you must be prepared at all times to talk with strangers about the informational or employment needs that motivated you to become involved in the networking process.

PREPARING TO NETWORK

In deliberately establishing relationships, maximize your efforts by organizing your approach. Five specific areas in which you can organize your efforts include reviewing your self-assessment, reviewing your research on job sites and organizations, deciding who it is you want to talk to, keeping track of all your efforts, and creating your self-promotion tools.

Review Your Self-Assessment

Your self-assessment is as important a tool in preparing to network as it has been in other aspects of your job search. You have carefully evaluated your personal traits, personal values, economic needs, longer-term goals, skill base, preferred skills, and underdeveloped skills. During the networking process you will be called upon to communicate what you know about yourself and relate it to the information or job you seek. Be sure to review the exercises that you completed in the self-assessment section of this book in preparation for networking. We've explained that you need to assess what skills you have acquired from your major that are of general value to an employer and to be ready to express those in ways employers can appreciate as useful in their own organizations.

Review Researching Job Sites and Organizations

In addition, individuals assisting you will expect that you'll have at least some background information on the occupation or industry of interest to you. Refer to the appropriate sections of this book and other relevant publications to acquire the background information necessary for effective networking. They'll explain how to identify not only the job titles that might be of interest to you, but also what kinds of organizations employ people to do that job. You will develop some sense of working conditions and expectations about duties and responsibilities—all of which will be of help in your networking interviews.

Decide Who It Is You Want to Talk To

Networking cannot begin until you decide who it is that you want to talk to and, in general, what type of information you hope to gain from your contacts. Once you know this, it's time to begin developing a list of contacts. Five useful sources for locating contacts are described here.

College Alumni Network.   Most colleges and universities have created a formal network of alumni and friends of the institution who are particularly interested in helping currently enrolled students and graduates of their alma mater gain employment-related information.

Because the computer major covers such a broad spectrum of human activity, you'll find computer graduates employed in every sector of the economy: government, business, and non-profit. The diversity of employment as evidenced by an alumni list from your college or university should be encouraging and informative to the computer graduate. Among a diverse group of alumni, there are likely to be scores of people you would enjoy talking with and even perhaps could meet.

It is usually a simple process to make use of an alumni network. You need only visit the alumni or career office at your college or university and follow the procedure that has been established. Often, you will simply complete a form indicating your career goals and interests and you will be given the names of appropriate individuals to contact. In many cases, staff members will coach you on how to make the best use of the limited time these alumni contacts may have available for you.

Alumni networkers may provide some combination of the following services: day-long shadowing experiences, telephone interviews, in-person interviews, information on relocating to given geographic areas, internship information, suggestions on graduate school study, and job vacancy notices.

What a valuable experience! Perhaps you are interested in working for a major corporation but are concerned about your degree preparation. Spending a day with an alumnus who works for a similar enterprise, asking lots of questions about his or her educational training and preparation, will give you a more concrete view of the possibilities for your degree. Observing firsthand how this person does the job will be an invaluable tool.

In addition to your own observations, the alumnus will have his or her own perspective on the relevance of your training and will give you realistic and honest feedback on your job search concerns.

Present and Former Supervisors. If you believe you are on good terms with present or former job supervisors, they may be an excellent resource for providing information or directing you to appropriate resources that would have information related to your current interests and needs. Additionally, these supervisors probably belong to professional organizations, which they might be willing to utilize to get information for you.

....

If, for example, you were interested in working as a computer programmer with a major department store chain and you are currently working as an assistant in a local retail shop, talk with your supervisor or the owner. He or she may belong to the Chamber of Commerce, whose director would have information on members affiliated with local branches of the chain. You would probably be able to obtain the names and telephone numbers of these people, thus enabling you to begin the networking process.

....

Employers in Your Area.   Although you may be interested in working in a geographic location different from the one where you currently reside, don't overlook the value of the knowledge and contacts those around you are able to provide. Use the local telephone directory and newspaper to identify the types of organizations you are thinking of working for or professionals who have the kinds of jobs you are interested in. Recently, a call made to a local hospital's financial administrator for information on working in health care financial administration yielded more pertinent information on training seminars, regional professional organizations, and potential employment sites than a national organization was willing to provide.

Employers in Geographic Areas Where You Hope to Work.   If you are thinking about relocating, identifying prospective employers or informational contacts in this new location will be critical to your success. Many resources are available to help you locate contact names. These include the yellow pages directory, the local newspapers, local or state business publications, and local Chambers of Commerce.

Professional Associations and Organizations.   Professional associations and organizations can provide valuable information in several areas: career paths that you may not have considered, qualifications relating to those career choices, publications that list current job openings, and workshops or seminars that will enhance your professional knowledge and skills. They can also be excellent sources for background information on given industries: their health, current problems, and future challenges.

There are several excellent resources available to help you locate professional associations and organizations that would have information to meet your needs. Two especially useful publications are the *Encyclopedia of Associations* and the *National Trade and Professional Associations of the United States.*

Keep Track of All Your Efforts

It can be difficult, almost impossible, to remember all the details related to each contact you make during the networking process, so you will want to develop a record-keeping system that works for you. Formalize this process by using a notebook or index cards to organize the information you gather. Begin by creating a list of the people or organizations you want to contact. Record the contact's name, address, telephone number, and what information you hope to gain. Each entry might look something like this:

Contact Name	Address	Phone #	Purpose
Mr. Tim Keefe	Wrigley Bldg.		
Dir. of Mines	Suite 72	555-8906	Resume screen

Once you have created this initial list, it will be helpful to keep more detailed information as you begin to actually make the contacts. Using the Network Contact Record form in Exhibit 4.1, keep good information on all your network contacts. They'll appreciate your recall of details of your meetings and conversations, and the information will help you to focus your networking efforts.

Exhibit 4.1

Network Contact Record

Name: Be certain your spelling is absolutely correct.

Title: Pick up a business card to be certain of the correct title.

Employing organization: Note any parent company or subsidiaries.

Business mailing address: This is often different from the street address.

Business telephone number: Include area code/alternative numbers/fax.

Source for this contact: Who referred you, and what is their relationship?

continued

---

continued

Date of call or letter: Use plenty of space here to record multiple phone calls or visits, other employees you may have met, names of secretaries/ receptionists, etc.

Content of discussion: Keep enough notes here to remind you of the substance of your visits and telephone conversations in case some time elapses between contacts.

Follow-up necessary to continue working with this contact:
Your contact may request that you send them some materials or direct you to contact an associate. Note any such instructions or assignments in this space.

Name of additional networker: Here you would record the names
Address: and phone numbers of additional
Phone: contacts met at this employer's
Name of additional networker: site. Often you will be introduced to
Address: many people, some of whom may
Phone: indicate a willingness to help in
Name of additional networker: your job search.
Address: ——————————————
Phone: ——————————————

Date thank-you note written: May help to date your next contact.

Follow-up action taken: Phone calls, visits, additional notes.

Other miscellaneous notes: Record any other additional interaction you may find is important to remember in working with this networking client. You will want this form in front of you when telephoning or just before and after a visit.

Create Your Self-Promotion Tools

There are two types of promotional tools that are used in the networking process. The first is a resume and cover letter, and the second is a one-minute "infomercial," which may be given over the telephone or in person.

Techniques for writing an effective resume and cover letter are covered in Chapter 2. Once you have reviewed that material and prepared these important documents, you will have created one of your self-promotion tools.

The one-minute infomercial will demand that you begin tying your interests, abilities, and skills to the people or organizations you want to network with. Think about your goal for making the contact to help you understand what you should say about yourself. You should be able to express yourself easily and convincingly. If, for example, you are contacting an alumna of your institution to obtain the names of possible employment sites in a distant city, be prepared to discuss why you are interested in moving to that location, the types of jobs you are interested in, and the skills and abilities you possess that will make you a qualified candidate.

To create a meaningful one-minute infomercial, write it out, practice it if it will be a spoken presentation, rewrite it, and practice it again if necessary until expressing yourself comes easily and is convincing.

Here's a simplified example of an infomercial for use over the telephone:

···

Hello, Mr. Kennedy? My name is Gary Sherman. I am a recent graduate of State College, and I wish to enter the health care field as a systems analyst. I feel confident that I have many of the skills I understand are valued for systems analysts in health care. I have a strong quantitative background, with good investigative and research skills. What's more, I have excellent interpersonal skills and work well under pressure. I understand these are valuable traits in this line of work!

Mr. Kennedy, I'm calling you because I still need more information about computer positions in the health care field. I'm hoping you'll have the time to sit down with me for about half an hour and discuss your perspective on careers in systems analysis. There are so many possible settings in which to work as a systems analyst and I am seeking some advice on which of those settings might be the best bet for my particular combination of skills and experience.

Would you be willing to do that for me? I would greatly appreciate it. I am available most mornings, if that's convenient for you.

···

Other effective self-promotion tools include portfolios for those in the arts, writing professions, or teaching. Portfolios show examples of work, photographs of projects or classroom activities, or certificates and credentials that are job related. There may not be an opportunity to use the portfolio during an interview, and it is not something that should be left with the organization. It is designed to be explained and displayed by the creator. However, during some networking meetings, there may be an opportunity to illustrate a point or strengthen a qualification by exhibiting the portfolio.

Beginning the Networking Process

Set the Tone for Your Contacts

It can be useful to establish "tone words" for any communications you embark upon. Before making your first telephone call or writing your first letter, decide what you want your contact to think of you. If you are networking to try to obtain a job, your tone words might include works like *genuine, informed,* and *self-knowledgeable.* When trying to acquire information, your tone words may have a slightly different focus, such as *courteous, organized, focused,* and *well spoken.* Use the tone words you establish for your contacts to guide you through the networking process.

Honestly Express Your Intentions

When contacting individuals, it is important to be honest about your reasons for making the contact. Establish your purpose in your own mind and be able and ready to articulate it concisely. Determine an initial agenda, whether it be informational questioning or self-promotion, present it to your contact, and be ready to respond immediately. If you don't adequately prepare before initiating your contacts, you may find yourself at a disadvantage if you're asked to immediately begin your informational interview or self-promotion during the first phone conversation or visit.

Start Networking within Your Circle of Confidence

Once you have organized your approach—by utilizing specific researching methods, creating a system for keeping track of the people you will contact, and developing effective self-promotion tools—you are ready to begin networking. The best place to begin networking is by talking with a group of people you trust and feel comfortable with. This group is usually made up of your family, friends, and career counselors. No matter who is in this inner circle, they will have a special interest in seeing you succeed in your job search. In addition, because they will be easy to talk to, you should try taking some risks in terms of practicing your information-seeking approach. Gain confidence in talking about the strengths you bring to an organization and the underdeveloped skills you feel hinder your candidacy. Be sure to review the section on self-assessment for tips on approaching each of these areas. Ask for critical but constructive feedback from the people in your circle of confidence on the letters you write and the one-minute infomercial you have developed. Evaluate whether you want to make the changes they suggest, then practice the changes on others within this circle.

Stretch the Boundaries of Your Networking Circle of Confidence

Once you have refined the promotional tools you will use to accomplish your networking goals, you will want to make additional contacts. Because you will not know most of these people, it will be a less comfortable activity to undertake. The practice that you gained with your inner circle of trusted friends should have prepared you to now move outside of that comfort zone.

It is said that any information a person needs is only two phone calls away, but the information cannot be gained until you (1) make a reasonable guess about who might have the information you need and (2) pick up the telephone to make the call. Using your network list that includes alumni, instructors, supervisors, employers, and associations, you can begin preparing your list of questions that will allow you to get the information you need. Review the question list shown below and then develop a list of your own.

Questions You Might Want to Ask

1. In the position you now hold, what do you do on a typical day?

2. What are the most interesting aspects of your job?

3. What part of your work do you consider dull or repetitious?

4. What were the jobs you had that led to your present position?

5. How long does it usually take to move from one step to the next in this career path?

6. What is the top position to which you can aspire in this career path?

7. What is the next step in *your* career path?

8. Are there positions in this field that are similar to your position?

9. What are the required qualifications and training for entry-level positions in this field?

10. Are there specific courses a student should take to be qualified to work in this field?

11. What are the entry-level jobs in this field?

12. What types of training are provided to persons entering this field?

13. What are the salary ranges your organization typically offers to entry-level candidates for positions in this field?

14. What special advice would you give a person entering this field?

15. Do you see this field as a growing one?

16. How do you see the content of the entry-level jobs in this field changing over the next two years?

17. What can I do to prepare myself for these changes?

18. What is the best way to obtain a position that will start me on a career in this field?

19. Do you have any information on job specifications and descriptions that I may have?

20. What related occupational fields would you suggest I explore?

21. How could I improve my resume for a career in this field?

22. Who else would you suggest I talk to, both in your organization and in other organizations?

Questions You Might Have to Answer

In order to communicate effectively, you must anticipate questions that will be asked of you by the networkers you contact. Review the list below and see if you can easily answer each of these questions. If you cannot, it may be time to revisit the self-assessment process.

1. Where did you get my name, or how did you find out about this organization?

2. What are your career goals?

3. What kind of job are you interested in?

4. What do you know about this organization and this industry?

5. How do you know you're prepared to undertake an entry-level position in this industry?

6. What course work have you taken that is related to your career interests?

7. What are your short-term career goals?

8. What are your long-term career goals?

9. Do you plan to obtain additional formal education?

10. What contributions have you made to previous employers?

11. Which of your previous jobs have you enjoyed the most, and why?

12. What are you particularly good at doing?

13. What shortcomings have you had to face in previous employment?

14. What are your three greatest strengths?

15. Describe how comfortable you feel with your communication style.

General Networking Tips

Make Every Contact Count. Setting the tone for each interaction is critical. Approaches that will help you communicate in an effective way include politeness, being appreciative of time provided to you, and being prepared and thorough. Remember, *everyone* within an organization has a circle of influence, so be prepared to interact effectively with each person you encounter in the networking process, including secretarial and support staff. Many information or job seekers have thwarted their own efforts by being rude to some individuals they encountered as they networked because they made the incorrect assumption that certain persons were unimportant.

Sometimes your contacts may be surprised at their ability to help you. After meeting and talking with you, they might think they have not offered much in the way of help. A day or two later, however, they may make a contact that would be useful to you and refer you to it.

With Each Contact, Widen Your Circle of Networkers. Always leave an informational interview with the names of at least two more people who can help you get the information or job that you are seeking. Don't be shy about asking for additional contacts; networking is all about increasing the number of people you can interact with to achieve your goals.

Make Your Own Decisions. As you talk with different people and get answers to the questions you pose, you may hear conflicting information or get conflicting suggestions. Your job is to listen to these "experts" and decide what information and which suggestions will help you achieve *your* goals. Only implement those suggestions that you believe will work for you.

SHUTTING DOWN YOUR NETWORK

As you achieve the goals that motivated your networking activity—getting the information you need or the job you want—the time will come to inactivate all or parts of your network. As you do so, be sure to tell your primary supporters about your change in status. Call or write to each one of them and give them as many details about your new status as you feel is necessary to maintain a positive relationship.

Because a network takes on a life of its own, activity undertaken on your behalf will continue even after you cease your efforts. As you get calls or are contacted in some fashion, be sure to inform these networkers about your change in status, and thank them for assistance they have provided.

Information on the latest employment trends indicates that workers will change jobs or careers several times in their lifetime. If you carefully and thoughtfully conduct your networking activities now, you will have solid experience when you need to network again.

CHAPTER FIVE

INTERVIEWING

ertainly, there can be no one part of the job search process more fraught with anxiety and worry than the interview. Yet seasoned job seekers welcome the interview and will often say, "Just get me an interview and I'm on my way!" They understand that the interview is crucial to the hiring process and equally crucial for them, as job candidates, to have the opportunity of a personal dialogue to add to what the employer may already have learned from a resume, cover letter, and telephone conversations.

Believe it or not, the interview is to be welcomed, and even enjoyed! It is a perfect opportunity for you, the candidate, to sit down with an employer and express yourself and display who you are and what you want. Of course, it takes thought and planning and a little strategy; after all, it *is* a job interview! But it can be a positive, if not pleasant, experience and one you can look back on and feel confident about your performance and effort.

For many new job seekers, a job, any job, seems a wonderful thing. But seasoned interview veterans know that the job interview is an important step for both sides—the employer and the candidate—to see what each has to offer and whether there is going to be a "fit" of personalities, work styles, and attitudes. And it is this concept of balance in the interview, that both sides have important parts to play, that holds the key to success in mastering this aspect of the job search strategy.

Try to think of the interview as a conversation between two interested and equal partners. You both have important, even vital, information to deliver and to learn. Of course, there's no denying the employer has some leverage, especially in the initial interview for recruitment or any interview scheduled by the candidate and not the recruiter. That should not prevent the interviewee from seeking to play an equal part in what should be a fair exchange of information. Too often the untutored candidate allows the interview to become one-sided. The employer asks all the questions and the candidate simply responds. The ideal would be for two mutually interested parties to sit down and discuss possibilities for each. For this is a *conversation of significance,* and it requires pre-interview preparation, thought about the tone of the interview, and planning of the nature and details of the information to be exchanged.

PREPARING FOR THE INTERVIEW

Most initial interviews are about 30 minutes long. Given the brevity, the information that is exchanged ought to be important. The candidate should be delivering material that the employer cannot discover on the resume and, in turn, the candidate should be learning things about the employer that he or she could not otherwise find out. After all, if you have only 30 minutes, why waste time on information that is already published? Not all the information exchanged is factual, and both sides will learn much from what they see of each other, as well. How the candidate looks, speaks, and acts is important to the employer. The employer's attention to the interview and awareness of the candidate's resume, the setting, and the quality of information presented are important to the candidate.

Just as the employer has every right to be disappointed when a prospect is late for the interview, looks unkempt, and seems ill-prepared to answer fairly standard questions, the candidate may be disappointed with an interviewer who isn't ready for the meeting, hasn't learned the basic resume facts, and is constantly interrupted for telephone calls. In either situation, there's good reason to feel let down.

There are many elements to a successful interview, and some of them are not easy to describe or prepare for. Sometimes there is just a chemistry between interviewer and interviewee that brings out the best in both, and a good exchange takes place. But there is much the candidate can do to pave the way for success in terms of his or her resume, personal appearance, goals, and interview strategy—each of which we will discuss. However, none of this preparation is as important as the time and thought the candidate gives to personal self-assessment.

Self-Assessment

Neither a stunning resume nor an expensive, well-tailored suit can compensate for candidates who do not know what they want, where they are going, or why they are interviewing with a particular employer. Self-assessment, the process by which we begin to know and acknowledge our own particular blend of education, experiences, needs, and goals is not something that can be sorted out the weekend before a major interview. Of all the elements of interview preparation, this one requires the longest lead time and cannot be faked.

Because the time allotted for most interviews is brief, it is all the more important for job candidates to understand and express succinctly why they are there and what they have to offer. This is not a time for undue modesty or for braggadocio, either; but it is a time for a compelling, reasoned statement of why you feel that you and this employer might make a good match. It means you have to have thought about your skills, interests, and attributes; related those to your life experiences and your own history of challenges and opportunities; and determined what that indicates about your strengths, preferences, values, and areas needing further development.

A common complaint of employers is that many candidates didn't take advantage of the interview time, didn't seem to know why they were there or what they wanted. When asked to talk about themselves and their work-related skills and attributes, employers don't want to be faced with shyness or embarrassed laughter; they need to know about you so they can make a fair determination of you and your competition. If you lose the opportunity to make a case for your employability, you can be certain the person ahead of you has or the person after you will, and it will be on the strength of those impressions that the employer will hire.

If you need some assistance with self-assessment issues, refer to Chapter 1. Included are suggested exercises that can be done as needed, such as making up an experiential diary and extracting obvious strengths and weaknesses from past experiences. These simple, pen-and-paper assignments will help you look at past activities as collections of tasks with accompanying skills and responsibilities. Don't overlook your high school or college career office, as well. Many offer personal counseling on self-assessment issues and may provide testing instruments such as the Myers-Briggs Type Indicator (MBTI)®, the Harrington-O'Shea Career Decision Making® System (CDM), the Strong Interest Inventory (SII)®, or any of a wide selection of assessment tools that can help you clarify some of these issues prior to the interview stage of your job search.

The Resume

Resume preparation has been discussed in detail, and some basic examples of various types were provided. In this section, we want to concentrate on how best to use your resume in the interview. In most cases, the employer will have seen the resume prior to the interview, and, in fact, it may well have been the quality of that resume that secured the interview opportunity.

An interview is a conversation, however, and not an exercise in reading. So, if the employer hasn't seen your resume and you have brought it along to the interview, wait until asked or until the end of the interview to offer it. Otherwise, you may find yourself staring at the back of your resume and simply answering "Yes" and "No" to a series of questions drawn from that document.

Sometimes an interviewer is not prepared and does not know or recall the contents of the resume and may use the resume to a greater or lesser degree as a "prompt" during the interview. It is for you to judge what that may indicate about the individual doing the interview or the employer. If your interviewer seems surprised by the scheduled meeting, relies on the resume to an inordinate degree, and seems otherwise unfamiliar with your background, this lack of preparation for the hiring process could well be a symptom of general management disorganization or may simply be the result of poor planning on the part of one individual. It is your responsibility as a potential employee to be aware of these signals and make your decisions accordingly.

....

In any event, it is perfectly acceptable for you to get the conversation back to a more interpersonal style by saying something like, "Mr. Smith, you might be interested in some recent programming experience I gained in an internship that is not detailed on my resume. May I tell you about it?" This can return the interview to two people talking to each other, not one reading and the other responding.

....

By all means, bring at least one copy of your resume to the interview. Occasionally, at the close of an interview, an interviewer will express an interest in circulating a resume to several departments, and you could then offer to provide those. Sometimes, an interview appointment provides an opportunity to meet others in the organization who may express an interest in you and your background, and it may be helpful to follow that up with a copy of your resume. Our best advice, however, is to keep it out of sight until needed or requested.

Appearance

Although many of the absolute rules that once dominated the advice offered to job candidates about appearance have now been moderated significantly, conservative is still the watchword unless you are interviewing in a fashion-related industry. For men, conservative translates into a well-cut dark suit with appropriate tie, hosiery, and dress shirt. A wise strategy for the male job seeker looking for a good but not expensive suit would be to try the men's department of a major department store. They usually carry a good range of sizes, fabrics, and prices; offer professional sales help; provide free tailoring; and have associated departments for putting together a professional look.

For women, there is more latitude. Business suits are still popular, but they have become more feminine in color and styling with a variety of jacket and skirt lengths. In addition to suits, better-quality dresses are now worn in many environments and, with the correct accessories, can be most appropriate. Company literature, professional magazines, the business section of major newspapers, and television interviews can all give clues about what is being worn in different employer environments.

Both men and women need to pay attention to issues such as hair, jewelry, and make-up; these are often what separates the candidate in appearance from the professional work force. It seems particularly difficult for the young job seeker to give up certain hair styles, eyeglass fashions, and jewelry habits, yet those can be important to the employer, who is concerned with your ability to successfully make the transition into the organization. Candidates often find the best strategy is to dress conservatively until they find employment. Once employed and familiar with the norms within your organization, you can begin to determine a look that you enjoy, works for you, and fits your organization.

Choose clothes that suit your body type, fit well, and flatter you. Feel good about the way you look! The interview day is not the best for a new hairdo, a new pair of shoes, or any other change that will distract you or cause you to be self-conscious. Arrive a bit early to avoid being rushed, and ask the receptionist to direct you to a restroom for any last-minute adjustments of hair and clothes.

Employer Information

Whether your interview is for graduate school admission, an overseas corporate position, or a reporter position with a local newspaper, it is important to know something about the employer or the organization. Keeping in mind that the interview is relatively brief and that you will hopefully have other interviews with other organizations, it is important to keep your research in proportion. If secondary interviews are called for, you will have additional time to do further research. For the first interview, it is helpful to know the organization's mission, goals, size, scope of operations, etc. Your research may uncover recent areas of challenge or particular successes that may help to fuel the interview. Use the "Where Are These Jobs, Anyway?" section of Chapter 3, your library, and your career or guidance office to help you locate this information in the most efficient way possible. Don't be shy in asking advice of these counseling and guidance professionals on how best to spend your preparation time. With some practice, you'll soon learn how much information is enough and which kinds of information are most useful to you.

INTERVIEW CONTENT

We've already discussed how it can help to think of the interview as an important conversation—one that, as with any conversation, you want to find pleasant and interesting and leaves you with a good feeling. But because this conversation is especially important, the information that's exchanged is critical to its success. What do you want them to know about you? What do you need to know about them? What interview technique do you need to particularly pay attention to? How do you want to manage the close of the interview? What steps will follow in the hiring process?

Except for the professional interviewer, most of us find interviewing stressful and anxiety-provoking. Developing a strategy before you begin interviewing will help you relieve some stress and anxiety. One particular strategy that has worked for many and may work for you is interviewing by objective. Before you interview, write down 3–5 goals you would like to achieve for that interview. They may be technique goals: smile a little more, have a firmer handshake, be sure to ask about the next stage in the interview process before I leave, etc. They may be content-oriented goals: find out about the company's current challenges and opportunities, be sure to speak of my recent research writing experiences or foreign travel, etc. Whatever your goals, jot down a few of them as goals for this interview.

Most people find that, in trying to achieve these few goals, their interviewing technique becomes more organized and focused. After the interview, the most common question friends and family ask is, "How did it go?" With this technique, you have an indication of whether you met *your* goals for the meeting, not just some vague idea of how it went. Chances are, if you accomplished what you wanted to, it informed the quality of the entire interview. As you continue to interview, you will want to revise your goals to continue improving your interview skills.

Now, add to the concept of the significant conversation the idea of a beginning, a middle, and a closing and you will have two thoughts that will give your interview a distinctive character. Be sure to make your introduction warm and cordial. Say your full name (and if it's a difficult-to-pronounce name, help the interviewer to pronounce it) and make certain you know your interviewer's name and how to pronounce it. Most interviews begin with some "soft talk" about the weather, chat about the candidate's trip to the interview site, national events, etc. This is done as a courtesy, to relax both you and the interviewer, to get you talking, and to generally try to defuse the atmosphere of excessive tension. Try to be yourself, engage in the conversation, and don't try to second-guess the interviewer. This is simply what it appears to be—casual conversation.

Once you and the interviewer move on to exchange more serious information in the middle part of the interview, the two most important concerns become your ability to handle challenging questions and your success at asking meaningful ones. Interviewer questions will probably fall into one of three categories: personal assessment and career direction, academic background, and knowledge of the employer. The following are some examples of questions in each category:

Personal Assessment and Career Direction

1. How would you describe yourself?

2. What motivates you to put forth your greatest effort?

3. In what kind of work environment are you most comfortable?

4. What do you consider to be your greatest strengths and weaknesses?

5. How well do you work under pressure?

6. What qualifications do you have that make you think you will be successful in this career?

7. Will you relocate? What do you feel would be the most difficult aspect of relocating?

8. Are you willing to travel?

9. Why should I hire you?

Academic Assessment

1. Why did you select your college or university?

2. What changes would you make at your alma mater?

3. What led you to choose your major?

4. What subjects did you like best and least? Why?

5. If you could, how would you plan your academic study differently? Why?

6. Describe your most rewarding college experience.

7. How has your college experience prepared you for this career?

8. Do you think that your grades are a good indication of your ability to succeed with this organization?

9. Do you have plans for continued study?

Knowledge of the Employer

1. If you were hiring a graduate of your school for this position, what qualities would you look for?

2. What do you think it takes to be successful in an organization like ours?

3. In what ways do you think you can make a contribution to our organization?

4. Why did you choose to seek a position with this organization?

The interviewer wants a response to each question but is also gauging your enthusiasm, preparedness, and willingness to communicate. In each response you should provide some information about yourself that can be related to the employer's needs. A common mistake is to give too much information. Answer each question completely, but be careful not to run on too long with extensive details or examples.

Questions about Underdeveloped Skills

Most employers interview people who have met some minimum criteria of education and experience. They interview candidates to see who they are, to learn what kind of personality they exhibit, and to get some sense of how this person might fit into the existing organization. It may be that you are asked about skills the employer hopes to find and that you have not documented. Maybe it's grant-writing experience, knowledge of the European political system, or a knowledge of the film world.

To questions about skills and experiences you don't have, answer honestly and forthrightly and try to offer some additional information about skills you do have. For example, perhaps the employer is disappointed you have no grant-writing experience. An honest answer may be as follows:

> No, unfortunately, I was never in a position to acquire those skills. I do understand something of the complexities of the grant-writing process and feel confident that my attention to detail, careful reading skills, and strong writing would make grants a wonderful challenge in a new job. I think I could get up on the learning curve quickly.

The employer hears an honest admission of lack of experience but is reassured by some specific skill details that do relate to grant writing and a confident manner that suggests enthusiasm and interest in a challenge.

For many students, questions about their possible contribution to an employer's organization can prove challenging. Because your education has probably not included specific training for a job, you need to review your academic record and select capabilities you have developed in your major that an employer can appreciate. For example, perhaps you read well and can analyze and condense what you've read into smaller, more focused pieces. That could be valuable. Or maybe you did some serious research and you know you have valuable investigative skills. Your public speaking might be highly developed and you might use visual aids appropriately and effectively. Or maybe your skill at correspondence, memos, and messages is effective. Whatever it is, you must take it out of the academic context and put it into a new, employer-friendly context so your interviewer can best judge how you could help the organization.

Exhibiting knowledge of the organization will, without a doubt, show the interviewer that you are interested enough in the available position to have done some legwork in preparation for the interview. Remember, it is not necessary to know every detail of the organization's history, but rather to have a general knowledge about why it is in business and how the industry is faring.

Sometime during the interview, generally after the midway point, you'll be asked if you have any questions for the interviewer. Your questions will tell the employer much about your attitude and your desire to understand the organization's expectations so you can compare it to your own strengths. The following are some selected questions you might want to ask:

1. What are the main responsibilities of the position?

2. What are the opportunities and challenges associated with this position?

3. Could you outline some possible career paths beginning with this position?

4. How regularly do performance evaluations occur?

5. What is the communication style of the organization? (meetings, memos, etc.)

6. Describe a typical day for me in this position.

7. What kinds of opportunities might exist for me to improve my professional skills within the organization?

8. What have been some of the interesting challenges and opportunities your organization has recently faced?

Most interviews draw to a natural closing point, so be careful not to prolong the discussion. At a signal from the interviewer, wind up your presentation, express your appreciation for the opportunity, and be sure to ask what the next stage in the process will be. When can you expect to hear from them? Will they be conducting second-tier interviews? If you're interested and haven't heard, would they mind a phone call? Be sure to collect a business card with the name and phone number of your interviewer. On your way out, you might have an opportunity to pick up organizational literature you haven't seen before.

With the right preparation—a thorough self-assessment, professional clothing, and employer information, you'll be able to set and achieve the goals you have established for the interview process.

CHAPTER SIX

NETWORKING OR INTERVIEWING FOLLOW-UP

uite often, there is a considerable time lag between interviewing for a position and being hired, or, in the case of the networker, between your phone call or letter to a possible contact and the opportunity of a meeting. This can be frustrating. "Why aren't they contacting me?" "I thought I'd get another interview, but no one has telephoned." "Am I out of the running?" You don't know what is happening.

CONSIDER THE DIFFERING PERSPECTIVES

Of course, there is another perspective—that of the networker or hiring organization. Organizations are complex, with multiple tasks that need to be accomplished each day. Hiring is but one discrete activity that does not occur as frequently as other job assignments. The hiring process might have to take second place to other, more immediate organizational needs. Although it may be very important to you and it is certainly ultimately significant to the employer, other issues such as fiscal management, planning and product development, employer vacation periods, or financial constraints, may prevent an organization or individual within that organization from acting on your employment or your request for information as quickly as you or they would prefer.

Use Your Communication Skills

Good communication is essential here to resolve any anxieties, and the responsibility is on you, the job or information seeker. Too many job seekers and networkers offer as an excuse that they don't want to "bother" the organization by writing letters or calling. Let us assure you here and now, once and for all, that if you are troubling an organization by over-communicating, someone will indicate that situation to you quite clearly. If not, you can only assume you are a worthwhile prospect and the employer appreciates being reminded of your availability and interest in them. Let's look at follow-up practices in both the job interview process and the networking situation separately.

Following Up on the Employment Interview

A brief thank-you note following an interview is an excellent and polite way to begin a series of follow-up communications with a potential employer with whom you have interviewed and want to remain in touch. It should be just that—a thank-you for a good meeting. If you failed to mention some fact or experience during your interview that you think might add to your candidacy, you may use this note to do that. However, this should be essentially a note whose overall tone is appreciative and, if appropriate, indicative of a continuing interest in pursuing any opportunity that may exist with that organization. It is one of the few pieces of business correspondence that may be handwritten, but always use plain, good-quality, monarch-size paper.

If, however, at this point you are no longer interested in the employer, the thank-you note is an appropriate time to indicate that. You are under no obligation to identify any reason for not continuing to pursue employment with that organization, but if you are so inclined to indicate your professional reasons (pursuing other employers more akin to your interests, looking for greater income production than this employer can provide, a different geographic location than is available, etc.), you certainly may. It should not be written with an eye to negotiation, for it will not be interpreted as such.

As part of your interview closing, you should have taken the initiative to establish lines of communication for continuing information about your candidacy. If you asked permission to telephone, wait a week following your thank-you note, then telephone your contact simply to inquire how things are progressing on your employment status. The feedback you receive here should be taken at face value. If your interviewer simply has no information, he or she will tell you so and indicate whether you should call again and when. Don't be discouraged if this should continue over some period of time.

If during this time something occurs that you think improves or changes your candidacy (some new qualification or experience you may have had), including any offers from other organizations, by all means telephone or write to inform the employer about this. In the case of an offer from a competing but less desirable or equally desirable organization, telephone your contact, explain what has happened, express your real interest in the organization, and inquire whether some determination on your employment might be made before you must respond to this other offer. If the organization is truly interested in you, they may be moved to make a decision about your candidacy. Equally possible is the scenario in which they are not yet ready to make a decision and so advise you to take the offer that has been presented. Again, you have no ethical alternative but to deal with the information presented in a straightforward manner.

When accepting other employment, be sure to contact any employers still actively considering you and inform them of your new job. Thank them graciously for their consideration. There are many other job seekers out there just like you who will benefit from having their candidacy improved when others bow out of the race. Who knows, you might, at some future time, have occasion to interact professionally with one of the organizations with whom you sought employment. How embarrassing to have someone remember you as the candidate who failed to notify them of taking a job elsewhere!

In all of your follow-up communications, keep good notes of who you spoke with, when you called, and any instructions that were given about return communications. This will prevent any misunderstandings and provide you with good records of what has transpired.

fOLLOWING uP ON THE nETWORK cONTACT

Far more common than the forgotten follow-up after an interview is the situation where a good network contact is allowed to lapse. Good communications are the essence of a network, and follow-up is not so much a matter of courtesy here as it is a necessity. In networking for job information and contacts, you are the active network link. Without you, and without continual contact from you, there is no network. You and your need for employment is often the only shared element between members of the network. Because network contacts were made regardless of the availability of any particular employment, it is incumbent upon the job seeker, if not simple common sense, that unless you stay in regular communication with the network, you will not be available for consideration should some job become available in the future.

This brings up the issue of responsibility, which is likewise very clear. The job seeker initiates network contacts and is responsible for maintaining those contacts; therefore, the entire responsibility for the network belongs with him or her. This becomes patently obvious if the network is left unattended. It very shortly falls out of existence, as it cannot survive without careful attention by the networker.

A variety of ways are open to you to keep the lines of communication open and to attempt to interest the network in you as a possible employee. You are limited only by your own enthusiasm for members of the network and your creativity. However, you as a networker are well-advised to keep good records of whom you have met and spoken with in each organization. Be sure to send thank-you notes to anyone who has spent any time with you, be it a quick tour of a department or a sit-down informational interview. All of these communications should, in addition to their ostensible reason, add some information about you and your particular combination of strengths and attributes.

You can contact your network at any time to convey continued interest, to comment on some recent article you came across concerning an organization, to add information about your training or changes in your qualifications, to ask advice or seek guidance in your job search, or to request referrals to other possible network opportunities. Sometimes just a simple note to network members reminding them of your job search, indicating that you have been using their advice, and noting that you are still actively pursuing leads and hope to continue to interact with them is enough to keep communications alive.

Because networks have been abused in the past, it's important that your conduct be above reproach. Networks are exploratory options, they are not back-door access to employers. The network works best for someone who is exploring a new industry or making a transition into a new area of employment and who needs to find information or to alert people to their search activity. Always be candid and direct with contacts in expressing the purpose of your call or letter and your interest in their help or information about their organization. In follow-up contacts, keep the tone professional and direct. Your honesty will be appreciated, and people will respond as best they can if your qualifications appear to meet their forthcoming needs. The network does not owe you anything, and that tone should be clear to each person you meet.

FEEDBACK FROM FOLLOW-UPS

A network contact may prove to be miscalculated. Perhaps you were referred to someone and it became clear that your goals and their particular needs did not make a good match. Or the network contact may simply not be in a position to provide you with the information you are seeking. Or in some unfortunate situations, the contact may become annoyed by being contacted for this purpose. In such a situation, many job seekers simply say "Thank you" and move on.

If the contact is simply not the right contact, but the individual you are speaking with is not annoyed by the call, it might be a better tactic to express regret that the contact was misplaced and then express to the contact what you are seeking and ask for their advice or possible suggestions as to a next step. The more people who are aware you are seeking employment, the better your chances of connecting, and that is the purpose of a network. Most people in a profession have excellent knowledge of their field and varying amounts of expertise on areas near to or tangent to their own. Use their expertise and seek some guidance before you dissolve the contact. You may be pleasantly surprised.

Occasionally, networkers will express the feeling that they have done as much as they can or provided all the information that is available to them. This may be a cue that they would like to be released from your network. Be alert to such attempts to terminate, graciously thank the individual by letter, and move on in your network development. A network is always changing, adding and losing members, and you want the network to be composed of only those who are actively interested in supporting your interests.

A Final Point on Networking for Computer Science Majors

In any of the settings a computer major might consider as a potential place to work, your contacts will be critically evaluating all of your written and oral communications. Pay particular attention to the quality of your interactions with people who are in a position to help you in your job search.

In your telephone communications, interview presentation, and follow-up correspondence, your warmth, style, and personality as evidenced in your spoken and written use of English will be part of the portfolio of impressions you create just as much as your computer ability is.

CHAPTER SEVEN

JOB OFFER CONSIDERATIONS

For many recent college graduates, the thrill of their first job and, for some, the most substantial regular income they have ever earned seems an excess of good fortune coming at once. To question that first income or be critical in any way of the conditions of employment at the time of the initial offer seems like looking a gift horse in the mouth. It doesn't seem to occur to many new hires even to attempt to negotiate any aspect of their first job. And, as many employers who deal with entry-level jobs for recent college graduates will readily confirm, the reality is that there simply isn't much movement in salary available to these new college recruits. The entry-level hire generally does not have an employment track record on a professional level to provide any leverage for negotiation. Real negotiations on salary, benefits, retirement provisions, etc., come to those with significant employment records at higher income levels.

Of course, the job offer is more than just money. It can be comprised of geographic assignment, duties and responsibilities, training, benefits, health and medical insurance, educational assistance, car allowance or company vehicle, and a host of other items. All of this is generally detailed in the formal letter that presents the final job offer. In most cases, this is a follow-up to a personal phone call from the employer representative who has been principally responsible for your hiring process.

That initial telephone offer is certainly binding as a verbal agreement, but most firms follow up with a detailed letter outlining the most significant parts of your employment contract. You may certainly choose to respond immediately at the time of the telephone offer (which would be considered a binding oral contract), but you will also be required to formally answer the letter of offer with a letter of acceptance, restating the salient elements of the employer's description of your position, salary, and benefits. This ensures that both parties are clear on the terms and conditions of employment and remuneration and any other outstanding aspects of the job offer.

Is This the Job You Want?

Most new employees will write this letter of acceptance back, glad to be in the position to accept employment. If you've worked hard to get the offer, and the job market is tight, other offers may not be in sight, so you will say "Yes, I accept!" What is important here is that the job offer you accept be one that does fit your particular needs, values, and interests as you've outlined them in your self-assessment process. Moreover, it should be a job that will not only use your skills and education, but also challenge you to develop new skills and talents.

Jobs are sometimes accepted too hastily, for the wrong reasons, and without proper scrutiny by the applicant. For example, an individual might readily accept a sales job only to find the continual rejection by potential clients unendurable. An office worker might realize within weeks the constraints of a desk job and yearn for more activity. Employment is an important part of our lives. It is, for most of our adult lives, our most continuous productive activity. We want to make good choices based on the right criteria.

If you have a low tolerance for risk, a job based on commission will certainly be very anxiety provoking. If being near your family is important, issues of relocation could present a decision crisis for you. If you're an adventurous person, a job with frequent travel would provide needed excitement and be very desirable. The importance of income, the need to continue your education, your personal health situation—all of these have an impact on whether the job you are considering will ultimately meet your needs. Unless you've spent some time understanding and thinking about these issues, it will be difficult to evaluate offers you do receive.

More importantly, if you make a decision that you cannot tolerate and feel you must leave that job, you will then have both unemployment and self-esteem issues to contend with. These will combine to make the next job search tough going, indeed. So make your acceptance a carefully considered decision.

Negotiating Your Offer

It may be that there is some aspect of your job offer that is not particularly attractive to you. Perhaps there is no relocation allotment to help you move your possessions and this presents some financial hardship for you. It may be that the medical and health insurance is less than you had hoped. Your initial assignment may be different than you expected, either in its location or in the duties and responsibilities that comprise it. Or it may simply be that the salary is less than you anticipated. Other considerations may be your official starting date of employment, vacation time, evening hours, dates of training programs or schools, etc.

If you are considering not accepting the job because of some item or items in the job offer "package" that do not meet your needs, you should know that most employers emphatically wish that you would bring that issue to their attention. It may be that the employer can alter it to make the offer more agreeable for you. In some cases, it cannot be changed. In any event, the employer would generally like to have the opportunity to try to remedy a difficulty rather than risk losing a good potential employee over an issue that might have been resolved. After all, they have spent time and funds in securing your services, and they certainly deserve an opportunity to resolve any possible differences.

Honesty is the best approach in discussing any objections or uneasiness you might have over the employer's offer. Having received your formal offer in writing, contact your employer representative and indicate your particular dissatisfaction in a straightforward manner. For example, you might explain that, while very interested in being employed by this organization, the salary (or any other benefit) is less than you have determined you require. State the terms you do need, and listen to the response. You may be asked to put this in writing, or you may be asked to hold off until the firm can decide on a response. If you are dealing with a senior representative of the organization, one who has been involved in hiring for some time, you may get an immediate response or a solid indication of possible outcomes.

Perhaps the issue is one of relocation. Your initial assignment is in the Midwest, and because you had indicated a strong West Coast preference, you are surprised at the actual assignment. You might simply indicate that, while you understand the need for the company to assign you based on its needs, you are disappointed and had hoped to be placed on the West Coast. You could inquire if that were still possible and, if not, would it be reasonable to expect a West Coast relocation in the future.

If your request is presented in a reasonable way, the employer will not see this as jeopardizing your offer. If they can agree to your proposal, they will. If not, they will simply tell you so, and you may choose to continue your candidacy with them or remove yourself from consideration as a possible employee. The choice will be up to you.

Some firms will adjust benefits within their parameters to meet the candidate's need if at all possible. If a candidate requires a relocation cost allowance, he or she may be asked to forgo tuition benefits for the first year to accomplish this adjustment. An increase in life insurance may be adjusted by some other benefit trade-off; perhaps a family dental plan is not needed. In these decisions, you are called upon, sometimes under time pressure, to know how you value these issues and how important each is to you.

Many employers find they are more comfortable negotiating for candidates who have unique qualifications or who bring especially needed expertise to the organization. Employers hiring large numbers of entry-level college graduates may be far more reluctant to accommodate any changes in offer conditions. They are well supplied with candidates with similar education and experience, so that if rejected by one candidate, they can draw new candidates from an ample labor pool.

COMPARING OFFERS

With only about 40 percent of recent college graduates employed three months after graduation, many graduates do not get to enjoy the experience of entertaining more than one offer at a time. The conditions of the economy, the job seekers' particular geographic job market, and their own needs and demands for certain employment conditions may not provide more than one offer at a time. Some job seekers may feel that no reasonable offer should go unaccepted, for the simple fear there won't be another.

In a tough job market, or if the job you seek is not widely available, or when your job search goes on too long and becomes difficult to sustain financially and emotionally, it may be necessary to accept an offer. The alternative is continued unemployment. Even here, when you feel you don't have a choice, you can at least understand that in accepting this particular offer, there may be limitations and conditions you don't appreciate. At the time of acceptance, there were no other alternatives, but the new employee can begin to use that position to gain the experience and talent to move toward a more attractive position.

Sometimes, however, more than one offer is received at one time, and the candidate has the luxury of choice. If the job seeker knows what he or she wants and has done the necessary self-assessment honestly and thoroughly, it may be clear that one of the offers conforms more closely to those expressed wants and needs.

However, if, as so often happens, the offers are similar in terms of conditions and salary, the question then becomes which organization might provide the necessary climate, opportunities, and advantages for your professional development and growth. This is the time when solid employer research and astute questioning during the interviews really pays off. How much did you learn about the employer through your own research and skillful questioning? When the interviewer asked during the interview, "Now, I'm sure you must have many questions?" did you ask the kinds of questions that would help resolve a choice between one organization and another? Just as an employer must decide among numerous applicants, so must the applicant learn to assess the potential employer. Both are partners in the job search.

RENEGING ON AN OFFER

An especially disturbing occurrence for employers and career counseling professionals is when a student formally (either orally or by written contract) accepts employment with one organization and later reneges on the agreement and goes with another employer.

There are all kinds of rationalizations offered for this unethical behavior. None of them satisfies. The sad irony is that what the job seeker is willing to do to the employer—make a promise and then break it—he or she would be outraged to have done to them—have the job offer pulled. It is a very bad way to begin a career. It suggests the individual has not taken the time to do the necessary self-assessment and self-awareness exercises to think and judge critically. The new offer taken may, in fact, be no better or worse than the one refused. Job candidates should be aware that there have been incidents of legal action following job candidates reneging on an offer. This adds a very sour note to what should be a harmonious beginning of a lifelong adventure.

CHAPTER EIGHT

THE GRADUATE SCHOOL CHOICE

he reasons for continuing one's education in graduate school can be as varied and unique as the individuals electing this course of action. Many continue their studies at an advanced level because they simply find it difficult to end the educational process. They love what they are learning and want to learn more and continue their academic exploration.

Continuing to work with a particular subject, such as the impact of artificial intelligence in an increasingly diverse workforce; and thinking, studying, researching, and writing critically on what others have discovered can provide excitement, challenge, and serious work. Some computer majors have loved this aspect of their academic work and want to continue that activity.

Others go on to graduate school for purely practical reasons; they have examined employment prospects in their field of study and all indications are that a graduate degree is requisite. If you have earned a B.S. in computer programming as a stepping stone to a career in upper-level management or systems analysis, for example, going on for further training becomes mandatory. As a bachelor's-level computer major, you realize you might not be able to move into more managerial positions without a master's degree. A review of jobs in different areas will suggest that at least a master's degree is important to be competitive. Alumni who are working in the government, for nonprofits, or in private industry can be a good source for finding out what degree level the different settings are hiring. Ask your college career office for some alumni names and give them a telephone call. Prepare some questions on specific job prospects in their field at each degree level. A thorough examination of the marketplace and talking to employers and professors will give you a sense of the scope of employment for a bachelor's degree, master's degree, or other related degree.

College teaching will require an advanced degree. The more senior executive positions in the career paths outlined in this book will require advanced training and perhaps a particular specialization in a subject area.

Consider Your Motives

The answer to the question of "Why graduate school?" is a personal one for each applicant. Nevertheless, it is important to consider your motives carefully. Graduate school involves additional time out of the employment market, a high degree of critical evaluation, significant autonomy as you pursue your studies, and considerable financial expenditure. For some students in doctoral programs, there may be additional life choice issues, such as relationships, marriage, and parenthood that may present real challenges while in a program of study. You would be well-advised to consider the following questions as you think about your decision to continue your studies.

Are You Postponing Some Tough Decisions by Going to School?

Graduate school is not a place to go to avoid life's problems. There is intense competition for graduate school slots and for the fellowships, scholarships, and financial aid available. This competition means extensive interviewing, resume submission, and essay writing that rivals corporate recruitment. Likewise, the graduate school process is a mentored one in which faculty stay aware of and involved in the academic progress of their students and continually challenge the quality of their work. Many graduate students are called upon to participate in teaching and professional writing and research as well.

In other words, this is no place to hide from the spotlight. Graduate students work very hard and much is demanded of them individually. If you elect to go to graduate school to avoid the stresses and strains of the "real world," you will find no safe place in higher academics. Vivid accounts, both fiction and nonfiction, have depicted quite accurately the personal and professional demands of graduate school work.

The selection of graduate studies as a career option should be a positive choice—something you *want* to do. It shouldn't be selected as an escape from other, less attractive or more challenging options, nor should it be selected as the option of last resort (i.e., "I can't do anything else; I'd better just stay in school"). If you're in some doubt about the strength of your reasoning about continuing in school, discuss the issues with a career counselor. Together you can clarify your reasoning, and you'll get some sound feedback on what you're about to undertake.

On the other hand, staying on in graduate school because of a particularly poor employment market and a lack of jobs at entry-level positions has proven to be an effective "stalling" strategy. If you can afford it, pursuing a graduate degree immediately after your undergraduate education gives you a year or two to "wait out" a difficult economic climate while at the same time acquiring a potentially valuable credential.

Have You Done Some "Hands-on" Reality Testing?

There are experiential options available to give some reality to your decision-making process about graduate school. Internships or work in the field can give you a good idea about employment demands, conditions, and atmosphere.

....

Graduate study is a viable choice for computer science majors who hope to enhance their careers. Publications such as *The Wall Street Journal's Managing Your Career* often contain articles about graduate training for computer professionals.

For computer science majors who want to take their education to a higher level with an eye toward college teaching, the need for some "hands-on" reality testing is vital. Talk with your college professors about their own educational and career paths as well as what their job actually entails, such as the time they spend outside the classroom, in research activities, or in departmental meetings.

Talking to people and asking questions is invaluable as an exercise to help you better understand the objective of your graduate study.

> For computer science majors especially, the opportunity to
> do this kind of reality testing helps to identify what your real-
> world skills are and how they can be put to use. Internships and
> co-op experiences speed up that process and prevent the frus-
> trating and expensive process of investigation many graduates
> begin only after graduation.

Do You Need an Advanced Degree to Work in Your Field?

Certainly there are fields such as law, psychiatry, medicine, and college teaching that demand advanced degrees. Is the field of employment you're considering one that also puts a premium on an advanced degree? You may be
surprised. Read the want ads in a number of major Sunday newspapers for
positions you would enjoy. How many of those require an advanced degree?

Retailing, for example, has always put a premium on what people can do, rather than how much education they have had. Successful people in retailing come
from all academic preparations. A Ph.D. in English may bring only prestige to the
individual employed as a magazine researcher. It may not bring a more senior position or better pay. In fact, it may disqualify you for some jobs because an employer might believe you will be unhappy to be overqualified for a particular position.
Or your motives in applying for the work may be misconstrued, and the employer
might think you will only be working at this level until something better comes
along. None of this may be true for you, but it comes about because you are working outside of the usual territory for that degree level.

When economic times are especially difficult, we tend to see stories fea-
tured about individuals with advanced degrees doing what is considered un-
suitable work, such as the Ph.D. in English driving a cab or the Ph.D. in
chemistry waiting tables. Actually, this is not particularly surprising when you
consider that as your degree level advances, the job market narrows apprecia-
bly. At any one time, regardless of economic circumstances, there are only so
many jobs for your particular level of expertise. If you cannot find employment for your advanced degree level, chances are you will be considered suspect for many other kinds of employment and may be forced into temporary
work far removed from your original intention.

Before making an important decision such as graduate study, learn your
options and carefully consider what you want to do with your advanced degree.
Ask yourself whether it is reasonable to think you can achieve your goals. Will there
be jobs when you graduate? Where will they be? What will they pay? How competitive will the market be at that time, based on current predictions?

If you're uncertain about the degree requirements for the fields you're interested in, you should check a publication such as the U.S. Department of
Labor's *Occupational Outlook Handbook*. Each entry has a section on training

and other qualifications that will indicate clearly what the minimum educational requirement is for employment, what degree is the standard, and what employment may be possible without the required credential.

For example, for physicists and astronomers, a doctoral degree in physics or a closely related field is essential. Certainly this is the degree of choice in academic institutions. However, the *Occupational Outlook Handbook* also indicates what kinds of employment may be available to individuals holding a master's or even a bachelor's degree in physics.

Have You Compared Your Expectations of What Graduate School Will Do for You with What It Has Done for Alumni of the Program You're Considering?

Most colleges and universities perform some kind of postgraduate survey of their students to ascertain where they are employed, what additional education they have received, and what levels of salary they are enjoying. Ask to see this information either from the university you are considering applying to or from your own alma mater, especially if it has a similar graduate program. Such surveys often reveal surprises about occupational decisions, salaries, and work satisfaction. This information may affect your decision.

The value of self-assessment (the process of examining and making decisions about your own hierarchy of values and goals) is especially important in this process of analyzing the desirability of possible career paths involving graduate education. Sometimes a job requiring advanced education seems to hold real promise but is disappointing in salary potential or numbers of opportunities available. Certainly, it is better to research this information before embarking on a program of graduate studies. It may not change your mind about your decision, but by becoming better informed about your choice, you become better prepared for your future.

Have You Talked with People in Your Field to Explore What You Might Be Doing after Graduate School?

In pursuing your undergraduate degree, you will have come into contact with many individuals trained in the field you are considering. You might also have the opportunity to attend professional conferences, workshops, seminars, and job fairs where you can expand your network of contacts. Talk to them all! Find out about their individual career paths, discuss your own plans and hopes, and get their feedback on the reality of your expectations, and heed their advice about your prospects. Each will have a unique tale to tell, and each will bring a different perspective on the current marketplace for the credentials you are seeking. Talking to enough people will make you an expert on what's out there.

Are You Excited by the Idea of Studying the Particular Field You Have in Mind?

This question may be the most important one of all. If you are going to spend several years in advanced study, perhaps engendering some debt or postponing some lifestyle decisions for an advanced degree, you simply ought to enjoy what you're doing. Examine your work in the discipline so far. Has it been fun? Have you found yourself exploring various paths of thought? Do you read in your area for fun? Do you enjoy talking about it, thinking about it, and sharing it with others? Advanced degrees often are the beginning of a lifetime's involvement with a particular subject. Choose carefully a field that will hold your interest and your enthusiasm.

It is fairly obvious by now that we think you should give some careful thought to your decision and take some action. If nothing else, do the following:

❑ Talk and question (remember to listen!)

❑ Reality-test

❑ Soul-search by yourself or with a person you trust

FINDING THE RIGHT PROGRAM FOR YOU: SOME CONSIDERATIONS

There are several important factors in coming to a sound decision about the right graduate program for you. You'll want to begin by locating institutions that offer appropriate programs, examining each of these programs and their requirements, undertaking the application process by obtaining catalogs and application materials, visiting campuses if possible, arranging for letters of recommendation, writing your application statement, and finally following up on your applications.

Locate Institutions with Appropriate Programs

Once you decide on a particular advanced degree, it's important to develop a list of schools offering such a degree program. Perhaps the best sources of graduate program information are Peterson's *Guides to Graduate Study.* Use these guides to build your list. In addition, you may want to consult the College Board's *Index of Majors and Graduate Degrees,* which will help you find graduate programs offering the degree you seek. It is indexed by academic major and then categorized by state.

Now, this may be a considerable list. You may want to narrow the choices down further by a number of criteria: tuition, availability of financial aid, public versus private institutions, U.S. versus international institutions, size of student body, size of faculty, application fee (this varies by school; most fall within the $10–$75 range), and geographic location. This is only a partial list; you will have your own important considerations. Perhaps you are an avid scuba diver and you find it unrealistic to think you could pursue graduate study for a number of years without being able to ocean dive from time to time. Good! That's a decision and it's honest. Now, how far from the ocean is too far, and what schools meet your other needs? In any case, and according to your own criteria, begin to build a reasonable list of graduate schools that you are willing to spend the time investigating.

Examine the Degree Programs and Their Requirements

Once you've determined the criteria by which you want to develop a list of graduate schools, you can begin to examine the degree program requirements, faculty composition, and institutional research orientation. Again, using a resource such as Peterson's *Guides to Graduate Study* can reveal an amazingly rich level of material by which to judge your possible selections.

In addition to degree programs and degree requirements, entries will include information about application fees, entrance test requirements, tuition, percentage of applicants accepted, numbers of applicants receiving financial aid, gender breakdown of students, numbers of full- and part-time faculty, and often gender breakdown of faculty as well. Numbers graduating in each program and research orientations of departments are also included in some entries. There is information on graduate housing, student services, and library, research, and computer facilities. A contact person, phone number, and address are also standard pieces of information in these listings. In addition to the standard entries, some schools pay an additional fee to place full-page, more detailed program descriptions. The location of such a display ad, if present, would be indicated at the end of the standard entry.

It can be helpful to draw up a chart and enter relevant information about each school you are considering in order to have a ready reference on points of information that are important to you.

Undertake the Application Process

The Catalog. Once you've decided on a selection of schools, send for catalogs and applications. It is important to note here that these materials might take many weeks to arrive. Consequently, if you need the materials quickly, it might be best to telephone and explain your situation to see whether the process can be speeded up for you. Also, check a local college or university library, which might have current and complete college catalogs in a microfiche collection. These microfiche copies can provide you with helpful information while you wait for your own copy of the graduate school catalog or bulletin to arrive.

When you receive your catalogs, give them a careful reading and make notes of issues you might want to discuss on the telephone or in a personal interview, if that's possible. Does the course selection have the depth you had hoped for?

···

If you are interested in graduate work in computer science, for example, in addition to classic courses such as theory and design, consider the availability of colloquiums, directed research opportunities, and specialized seminars.

···

What is the ratio of faculty to the required number of courses for your degree? How often will you encounter the same faculty member as an instructor?

If, for example, your program offers a practicum or off-campus experience, who arranges this? Does the graduate school select a site and place you there, or is it your responsibility? What are the professional affiliations of the faculty? Does the program merit any outside professional endorsement or accreditation?

Critically evaluate the catalogs of each of the programs you are considering. List any questions you have and ask current or former teachers and colleagues for their impressions as well.

The Application.   Preview each application thoroughly to determine what you need to provide in the way of letters of recommendation, transcripts from undergraduate schools or any previous graduate work, and personal essays that may be required. Make a notation for each application of what you need to complete that document.

Additionally, you'll want to determine entrance testing requirements for each institution and immediately arrange to complete your test registration. For example, the Graduate Record Exam (GRE) and the Graduate Management Admission Test (GMAT) each have 3–4 weeks between the last registration date and the test date. Your local college career office should be able to provide you with test registration booklets, sample test materials, information on test sites and dates, and independent test review materials that might be available commercially.

Visit the Campus If Possible

If time and finances allow, a visit, interview, and tour can help make your decision easier. You can develop a sense of the student body, meet some of the faculty, and hear up-to-date information on resources and the curriculum. You will have a brief opportunity to "try out" the surroundings to see if they fit your needs. After all, it will be home for a while. If a visit is not possible but you have questions, don't hesitate to call and speak with the dean of the graduate school. Most are more than happy to talk to candidates and want them to have the answers they seek. Graduate school admission is a very personal and individual process.

Arrange for Letters of Recommendation

This is also the time to begin to assemble a group of individuals who will support your candidacy as a graduate student by writing letters of recommendation or completing recommendation forms. Some schools will ask you to provide letters of recommendation to be included with your application or sent directly to the school by the recommender. Other graduate programs will provide a recommendation form that must be completed by the recommender. These graduate school forms vary greatly in the amount of space provided for a written recommendation. So that you can use letters as you need to, ask your recommenders to address their letters "To Whom It May Concern," unless one of your recommenders has a particular connection to one of your graduate schools or knows an official at the school.

Choose recommenders who can speak authoritatively about the criteria important to selection officials at your graduate school. In other words, choose recommenders who can write about your grasp of the literature in your field of study, your ability to write and speak effectively, your class performance, and your demonstrated interest in the field outside of class. Other characteristics that graduate schools are interested in assessing include your emotional maturity, leadership ability, breadth of general knowledge, intellectual ability, motivation, perseverance, and ability to engage in independent inquiry.

When requesting recommendations, it's especially helpful to put the request in writing. Explain your graduate school intentions and express some of your thoughts about graduate school and your appreciation for their support. Don't be shy about "prompting" your recommenders with some suggestions of what you would appreciate being included in their comments. Most recommenders will find this direction helpful and will want to produce a statement of support that you can both stand behind. Consequently, if your interaction with one recommender was especially focused on research projects, he or she might be best able to speak of those skills and your critical thinking ability. Another recommender may have good comments to make about your public presentation skills.

Give your recommenders plenty of lead time in which to complete your recommendation, and set a date by which they should respond. If they fail to meet your deadline, be prepared to make a polite call or visit to inquire if they need more information or if there is anything you can do to move the process along.

Whether or not you are providing a graduate school form or asking for an original letter to be mailed, be sure to provide an envelope and postage if the recommender must mail the form or letter directly to the graduate school.

Each recommendation you request should provide a different piece of information about you for the selection committee. It might be pleasant for letters of recommendation to say that you are a fine, upstanding individual, but a selection committee for graduate school will require specific information. Each recommender has had a unique relationship with you, and their letters should reflect that. Think of each letter as helping to build a more complete portrait of you as a potential graduate student.

Write Your Application Statement

> For the computer major, the application and personal essay should be a welcome opportunity to express your deep interest in pursuing graduate study. Your understanding of the challenges ahead, your commitment to the work involved, and your expressed self-awareness will weigh heavily in the decision process of the graduate school admissions committee.

An excellent source to help in thinking about writing this essay is *How to Write a Winning Personal Statement for Graduate and Professional School* by Richard J. Stelzer. It has been written from the perspective of what graduate school selection committees are looking for when they read these essays. It provides helpful tips to keep your essay targeted on the kinds of issues and criteria that are important to selection committees and that provide them with the kind of information they can best utilize in making their decision.

Follow Up on Your Applications

After you have finished each application and mailed it along with your transcript requests and letters of recommendation, be sure to follow up on the progress of your file. For example, call the graduate school administrative staff to see whether your transcripts have arrived. If the school required your recommenders to fill out a specific recommendation form that had to be mailed directly to the school, you will want to ensure that they have all arrived in good time for the processing of your application. It is your responsibility to make certain that all required information is received by the institution.

RESEARCHING FINANCIAL AID SOURCES, SCHOLARSHIPS, AND FELLOWSHIPS

Financial aid information is available from each school, so be sure to request it when you call for a catalog and application materials. There will be several lengthy forms to complete, and these will vary by school, type of school (public versus private), and state. Be sure to note the deadline dates for these important forms.

There are many excellent resources available to help you explore all of your financial aid options. Visit your college career office or local public library to find out about the range of materials available. Two excellent resources include Peterson's *Grants for Graduate Students* and the Foundation Center's *Foundation Grants to Individuals*. These types of resources generally contain information that can be accessed by indexes including field of study, specific eligibility requirements, administering agency, and geographic focus.

EVALUATING ACCEPTANCES

If you apply to and are accepted at more than one school, it is time to return to your initial research and self-assessment to evaluate your options and select the program that will best help you achieve the goals you set for pursuing graduate study. You'll want to choose a program that will allow you to complete your studies in a timely and cost-effective way. This may be a good time to get additional feedback from professors and career professionals who are familiar with your interests and plans. Ultimately, the decision is yours, so be sure you get answers to all the questions you can think of.

SOME NOTES ABOUT REJECTION

Each graduate school is searching for applicants who appear to have the qualifications necessary to succeed in its program. Applications are evaluated on a combination of undergraduate grade point average, strength of letters of recommendation, standardized test scores, and personal statements written for the application.

A carelessly completed application is one reason many applicants are denied admission to a graduate program. To avoid this type of needless rejection, be sure to carefully and completely answer all appropriate questions on the application form, focus your personal statement given the instructions provided, and submit your materials well in advance of the deadline. Remember that your test scores and recommendations are considered a part of your application, so they must also be received by the deadline.

If you are rejected by a school that especially interests you, you may want to contact the dean of graduate studies to discuss the strengths and weaknesses of your application. Information provided by the dean will be useful in reapplying to the program or applying to other, similar programs.

PART TWO

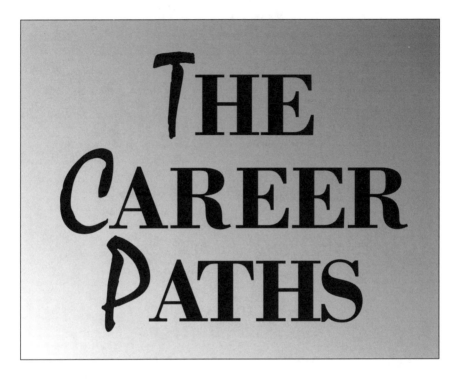

THE CAREER PATHS

CHAPTER NINE

INTRODUCTION TO THE COMPUTER SCIENCE CAREER PATHS

"Technology improves things so fast that by the time we can afford the best, there's something better."

—Anonymous

Very few aspects of everyday life have been left untouched by the computer revolution. When you buy something at the store, most likely your purchase will be scanned at the checkout counter by a reader of UPC bar codes. Bring a package to your local post office to mail, and the clerk will put it on a scale that is attached to a computer terminal. After the clerk inputs some information by pressing a few buttons, the computer's display tells you exactly how much the package will cost to mail. CAT scans help doctors view kidneys, hearts, and other body organs to see if they are healthy. Farmers rely on computers to plan planting and harvesting of crops. Every time you reserve space on an airplane, check your bank statement, or phone a friend, you are depending on computers.

With this tremendous growth has come an accompanying demand for personnel in the computer industry—all types at all levels, but for the most part, people skilled in computer science—to handle jobs both within and outside the industry. People are needed to handle such tasks as design and engineering of computer hardware and software, and in sales and service, systems development and programming, and computer operations.

Predicting what lies in the future is virtually impossible, but we do know that whatever it brings, computer technology will be right in the center of it. As computer technology continues to advance and develop for both home and industry, there will be an ever-growing need for computer professionals to fill the resulting job openings. Career opportunities in the computer field will remain strong, and knowledge of computer technology will continue to become more and more important to workers in every field.

Career paths in computer-related fields are as diverse as the applications of computer technology. A vast number of avenues are open to computer science graduates, and it's hard to know where to begin in describing them. This book is designed to help you sort out your options in order to make an intelligent decision about your future.

In This Book

Though this book does not provide information about every career in the world of computer science, the chapters that follow offer an abundance of information about many careers in this field. Though there are overlapping duties and responsibilities for those who perform many of the jobs, individuals in this field all have one element in common—a love for solving problems and making life better through the use of computers.

The six career paths described in this book include:

❏ Path 1. Computer Scientists and Systems Analysts

❏ Path 2. Management Analysts and Consultants

❏ Path 3. Operations Research Analysts

❏ Path 4. Computer Operators and Programmers

❏ Path 5. Computer Sales and Service

❏ Path 6. Other Computer Science Careers

Computer science is a vast field that provides many opportunities for those who are willing to prepare themselves and work hard to achieve success. Read on to determine which area of computer science appeals to you most and then take the necessary steps to fulfill your dream.

*"Far and away the best
prize that life offers is the
chance to work hard at
work worth doing."*

—Theodore Roosevelt

CHAPTER TEN

PATH 1: COMPUTER SCIENTISTS AND SYSTEMS ANALYSTS

"Computers are useless. They can only give you answers."

—Pablo Picasso

HELP WANTED

Computer Scientists and Engineers

We are a high technology company specializing in state-of-the-art software engineering and computer services. We are seeking high quality computer scientists and engineers for our southwest Washington location. Bachelor of Science Degree in Engineering, Computer Science, or a related field. Excellent benefits/relocation package.

Requires any of the following skills:

MS Access, Visual Basic, SQL

C4I with software skills

Oracle 7.x, Forms 4.5, CASE tools

C/C++ in Windows 95/NT or Motif environment

Ada, C, X Windows/Motif on UNIX-based systems

continued

> continued
>
> C/C++, FORTRAN, Telemetry, VMS, UNIX
>
> C/C++, UNIX, OLE/CMM/2167A
>
> Visual C++, Windows 95, MSFC
>
> Must be U.S. citizen and meet eligibility requirements for access to classified information. We are a drug free workplace. Send resume with salary requirements in strictest confidence.

The above is a typical ad you might expect to find in a city newspaper. It is genuine, as are all of the want ads included in this book. Each one provides insights into the kinds of professionals employers are seeking and also reveals information about qualifications, work expectations, and compensation. The want ads allow you to peek into the world of computers. Perhaps you will decide that it is the world you will choose to make your career.

DEFINITION OF THE CAREER PATH

Computers—it's hard to imagine a world without them. As a result of new technologies, particularly in the past twenty years or so, our modern society has been almost deluged by a continual introduction of new products, both in computer hardware systems and software.

The manufacturing of computer hardware includes all the components, such as the CPU (central processing unit) and peripheral equipment such as disks, monitors, storage devices, tape drives, and printers.

Computer software consists of a program or programs made up of machine-readable instructions that perform a logical sequence of functions—anything from maintaining a bookkeeping system to performing computer games.

All of the remarkable and continuing advances in computer technology may be credited to the highly trained and skilled group of professionals called computer scientists. This group includes computer designers, software designers, computer engineers, product designers, systems analysts, computer support analysts, and database managers and administrators.

Computer Scientist

Computer scientists conduct research, design computers, and discover and use principles of applied computer technology. Though they may perform many of the same duties as other computer professionals, their jobs are distinguished by the higher level of theoretical expertise they apply to complex problems and the innovative ideas for the application or creation of new technology.

Computer professionals who are employed by academic institutions work in areas from theory, to hardware, to language design, or to multi-disciplinary projects; for example, developing and advancing uses for artificial intelligence (AI). Their counterparts in private industry work in areas such as applying theory, developing specialized languages, or design-ing programming tools, knowledge-based systems, or computer games.

HELP WANTED

Computer Scientist

Description:

We are one of the world's largest and most diversified industrial laboratories. The cornerstone of our commitment to technical leadership, along with the advanced innovations and technical expertise produced here, have benefited a broad and diverse range of areas from the information revolution to the environ-ment, from financial services to advanced materials. The results are a myriad of progressive inventions and discoveries that continue to help businesses develop future generation products and processes. We currently have the following opportunity:

Computer Scientist

Responsibilities:

Carry out ongoing research programs, for example, automated fingerprint analysis and scene reconstruction. Develop new Research and Development (R&D) applications in support of our businesses. Publish and carry out professional activities in the field of Computer Vision.

Requirements:

Ph.D. in Computer Science with Computer Vision Specialty. At least one year of postdoctoral experience, working in Computer Vision and Image Understanding.

Desired:

Experience working in Fingerprint Analysis and Matching, 3D Modeling, and Site Model Exploitation.

We offer a competitive salary, outstanding benefits package, and the professional advantages of an environment that sup-ports your development and recognizes your achievements. For consideration, please send or fax your resume.

Computer Designer

Designers in the computer industry are responsible for researching and developing new computer hardware products. They analyze data to determine the feasibility of a product, work with other research personnel to develop a detailed description of the product, and plan and develop experimental test programs to determine the success or failure of their designs.

Computer Product Design Engineer

Computer product design engineers work alongside designers. Together they are responsible for developing new computer hardware products.

Computer engineers concentrate on the hardware and software aspects of systems design and development, assist designers in the development of specifications, and supervise other engineers. They often work as part of a team that designs new computing devices or computer-related equipment.

Software Engineer

Software engineers focus their efforts on maintaining, enhancing, and/or debugging existing software. They may also see to it that computer systems are operating properly and create new software programs.

HELP WANTED

Software Engineer

National specialty managed care company seeking an individual with a strong technical background in client/server application coding and database administration and design. The individual should have a Bachelor's Degree in Computer Science or a related field, a minimum of three years experience using SQL Windows, C, and working with a relational database.

Software Developer

Software developers produce computer-based products (both packaged and systems software) and services for both individual consumers and corporations. They coordinate the production of software products, from choosing content providers, assembling graphics creators, and working with programmers, through the actual assembling, pressing, and distribution of the end product. Much of a software developer's day is spent on the telephone in an attempt to coordinate the production with other members of the working team. These professionals report that there is a feeling of pride in creating something that didn't exist previously.

HELP WANTED

Software Application Developers

Responsibilities include developing our next generation of Manufacturing Application Software. Duties will include the design and development of enhanced requirements, planning, and scheduling software products in a client/server environment.

Requirements include a bachelor's degree or equivalent experience, strong C programming skills, and manufacturing software development experience, particularly MRP or Production Scheduling. Preference will be given to candidates with experience in Optimization, Finite Capacity Scheduling, or Constraining-Based Planning/Scheduling. Memory Resident Programming experience and/or CASE tool knowledge are also a plus.

Software Designer

Software designers are the researchers who create the operating systems that allow users to interface with the computer. In addition, they create the software products that perform specific functions or applications such as word processing packages.

Software designers assess needs, create a chart showing how the program will work, and determine the components that will appear on each screen. Then, based on the customer's existing equipment or preferences, they devise compatible software. Software designers also update, debug, and modify existing programs.

HELP WANTED

Software Design Engineer

Our company is growing—come join the team!

Design, develop, and implement software for Real Time Operating Systems. Qualified candidates will have a Bachelor of Science Degree in Computer Science or a related field and experience with Real Time Operating Systems, Developing Communications Protocols, and Operating Systems (C, C++ preferred).

We are a high technology electronic engineering designer of real time single board computers. End users of our products require flexible capability, exceptional reliability, high speed processing

continued

> continued
>
> capacity, and deterministic computer response time, particularly in communications applications. Excellent benefits and casual work environment.

Computer Database Manager/Administrator

Computer database managers and database administrators design, write, and oversee computer database systems in an effort to make sure that the right person can access the right information at the right time. Their main responsibilities include maintaining the efficiency of the database in addition to the following:

1. Organizing the information into a computer file

2. Watching over the system to make sure that users do not tamper with the information or the system structure (the way it is put together)

3. Making or approving all changes or modifications to the database information or program

Computer Database Managers and Administrators may also be responsible for maintaining the security of their systems.

HELP WANTED

Database Services Manager

Direct marketing technology has led the industry in applying computer-based services and leading-edge information management techniques for direct marketers. Our database services area helps clients maintain records of customers, orders, and promotions. From a simple file update to a complex relational design, we develop and implement efficient database solutions. The manager of our database team will manage marketing databases for clients, provide client services, and direct updating and reporting performed to meet the client's requests. The manager will also hire, develop, and review staff, troubleshoot, develop documentation, and set production schedules.

A bachelor's degree or equivalent, 4 years direct marketing or database experience, and supervisory skills required. MVS and DB2 or other relational database experience preferred. We offer a competitive salary and benefits package.

HELP WANTED

Database Administrator

We are an energy oriented research management organization committed to developing safe, useful products for the natural gas industry and its customers.

You will be responsible for administering our Oracle 7.x database system and PeopleSoft applications running on a Windows NT platform. This will encompass server configuration, system integration and testing, data modeling, end-user support, database tuning and troubleshooting, installations, and performance enhancements.

We require 5+ years of involvement with information technologies and 2+ years of system administration, database administration, and database development experience in a mission-critical environment. Knowledge of Oracle 7.x, Windows NT 3.51 or 4.0, Oracle tools, SQL, report writer and client/server applications is essential. Strong problem-solving, communication, and analytical skills are also expected. Exposure to Internet/Intranet, Lotus Notes, and PeopleSoft applications would be ideal.

Computer Support Analyst

Computer support analysts are responsible for providing assistance and advice to users, interpreting problems, and providing technical support for hardware, software, and systems. They may be employed by organizations or computer or software vendors.

Systems Analyst

HELP WANTED

Systems Analyst

Our state university invites nominations and applications for a systems analyst position. This position is an outstanding opportunity for the highly motivated, serious programmer desiring experience with exciting technology. A Bachelor's Degree in Computer Science or related field from a regionally accredited institution is required. Professional experience in object-oriented programming and SQL applications is preferred. Professional programming

continued

---

continued

experience in an IBM/MVS mainframe environment is required. Experience with Internet and/or Webserver development, DOS, UNI, OS/2, Windows, Powerbuilder, Novell netware, ADS/O, CICS, IDMS, and IBM JCL is preferred.

This position provides the opportunity to work with the latest technologies. Assignments may include projects such as developing and/or installing and maintaining client/server application systems for the university library, providing SQL applications and reports for administrative departments, or developing mainframe solutions in existing administrative systems. Interpersonal relationship skills are essential to work with and train administrative users. The Systems Analyst will receive assignments and technical supervision from the Administrative Programming Manager.

Applications must include a letter which specifically addresses how skills, education, and experience relate to the position announcement. Also include a resume and a list of three references.

About 400,000 individuals are employed as systems analysts—professionals who are hired to define business, scientific, or engineering problems and design their solutions using computers. Systems analysts may design entirely new systems, including hardware and software, or add a single new software application to harness more of the computer's power.

Architects of the computer team, systems analysts begin their work by meeting with various individuals who are involved in the project. For instance, the Internal Revenue Service might seek a new system designed to process tax returns, but the auditors and accountants don't know how to go about setting this up, so they will seek the aid of a systems analyst.

Much time is devoted to clearly defining the goals of the system so that it can be broken down into separate programmable procedures. Through the use of techniques such as structured analysis, data modeling, information engineering, and cost accounting, systems analysts map out the new system. Once the design has been developed, systems analysts prepare charts and diagrams that describe it in terms that managers and other users can understand. Following this, systems analysts often prepare a cost-benefit and return-on-investment analysis to help management decide whether the proposed system will be satisfactory to meet their needs.

After this study is completed, analysts translate the requirements of the existing system into the capabilities of a computer system. They then prepare specifications for programmers to follow so that they can accurately write the programs necessary to make the computer system function as required.

Some organizations do not employ programmers; instead a single worker called a programmer/analyst is responsible for both systems analysis and programming.

HELP WANTED

Programmer/Systems Analyst

Our manufacturing company with multiple locations is upgrading to a UNIX environment using HP hardware and operating system. We will also be implementing the MFG/PRO and Progress software business system. To facilitate this growth, we are currently seeking a programmer/systems analyst.

The ideal candidate will have a bachelor's degree, knowledge of HP hardware and operating systems and have two years programming experience using Progress software. Experience with Word, Excel, and other Microsoft products required. Current certified Novell administrator is preferred, with EDI and/or bar code experience a plus. In return, we offer a comprehensive compensation and benefits package.

Some analysts become involved with every conceivable type of system. A business systems analyst may work with accounts receivable, accounts payable, inventory, general ledger, payroll, or any other type of business system. A scientific or engineering systems analyst may work for NASA, for example, on a system that analyzes stresses on steel beams or a system that is designed to send a man or woman to the moon.

Because up-to-date information—accounting records, sales figures, or budget projections, for example—is so important in modern organizations, systems analysts may be instructed to make the computer systems in each department compatible with one other so that facts and figures can be shared. Similarly, electronic mail requires open pathways to send messages, documents, and data from one computer "mailbox" to another across different equipment and program lines. Analysts must design the hardware and software to allow free exchange of data, custom applications, and the computer power to process it all. They study the seemingly incompatible pieces and create ways to link them so that users can access information from any part of the system.

HELP WANTED

Internet/Intranet Systems Analyst

In 71 countries, for over 8000+ corporate clients utilizing our proprietary products, we've built one of the software industry's greatest success stories. We're the world's leading developer/ provider of cost-effective business enterprise information systems to the industrial sector. Our commitment to continued success/growth is substantial. We're opening new offices, entering new markets, investing millions in both R&D (Research and Development) and capital expenditures. And we're hiring the best professionals worldwide. Now we're inviting you to be a part of the biggest, boldest plans ever.

Job responsibilities include developing and implementing global Internet and Intranet solutions for support of our corporate clients and staff worldwide. The candidate's primary job responsibilities will be Windows NT domain administration and merging Web and database technologies.

Key requirements include a BS/BA in Computer Science/Information Systems and 1+ years experience with one or more of the following: C++, Visual Basic, HTML, Java, DOS, Windows 3.x, Windows 95, Web Site development and/or implementation, Windows NT 3.51 and 4.0 Domain Administration, and MS Access Database. Prefer experience (though not required) in: Electronic publishing or journalism/writing, UNIX systems administration, Hypertext linking, Lotus Notes, Informix or Oracle, Novell CAN, or graphic design.

POSSIBLE JOB TITLES

Computer database administrator	Computer support analyst
	Internet developer
Computer database manager	Software applications
Computer designer	developer
Computer engineer	Software designer
Computer product design engineer	Software developer
	Software engineer
Computer scientist	Systems analyst

HELP WANTED

Systems Analysts

Make the most of your talent by joining our team!

Knowledgeable? Energetic? Are you looking for a challenging position that opens up a world of career opportunities? These are the kinds of people we are searching for to join our team. We want you to help us in developing mission critical solutions using state-of-the-art technology, while making the most of your skills and broadening your expertise.

As a Systems Analyst you will help define user requirements and systems specifications for manufacturing, distribution, and retail financial applications. To qualify, you must have at least five years of IS (Information Systems) experience which should include prior programming and development experience, as well as exposure to entity, data, and process modeling. Strong platform and workshop facilitation skills are preferred, along with broad-based knowledge of business operations.

POSSIBLE EMPLOYERS

At present, approximately 828,000 professionals are employed as computer scientists and systems analysts. Although they can be found in small offices and most industries (manufacturing, banking, hospitals, travel, and hospitality, for example), the greatest concentration is in the computer and data processing services industry. This includes firms that design and install computer systems; integrate or network systems; perform data processing and database management; develop packaged software; and even operate entire computer facilities under contract. Many others work for government agencies (particularly in the armed forces), for manufacturers of computers and related electronic equipment, for insurance companies, and for universities.

A growing number of computer scientists and systems analysts are employed on a temporary or contract basis. For example, a company installing a new computer system may need the services of several systems analysts to get their systems up and running, but these professionals would only be needed temporarily. Such jobs may last from several months up to two years or more.

RELATED OCCUPATIONS

Other workers who use research, logic, and creativity to solve business problems are:

Actuary	Manufacturing and product
Computer programmer	development professional
Consultant	Operations research analyst
Electronic publishing	Professional involved in
professional	translation services for
Engineer	annual reports
Financial analyst	Programmer
Management analyst	Urban planner
Manager	

HELP WANTED

Systems Analyst
Your solid background in hands-on application development combined with good communications and interpersonal skills will allow you to excel in technical projects with possibilities for eventual advancement to a leadership role. Requires solid problem-solving, writing, and organizational skills to supplement technical expertise in COBOL, JCL, CICS, DB2, and MVS. Visual Gen is a plus. Insurance industry knowledge or background is highly desired.

WORKING CONDITIONS

Computer scientists and systems analysts usually enjoy a pleasant working environment in comfortable surroundings in offices or laboratories amid state-of-the-art equipment. Given the technology available today, more work, including technical support, can be done from remote locations using modems, laptops, electronic mail, and even through the Internet.

These technical professionals usually work independently, about 40 hours a week, the same as many other professional or office workers. Occasionally projects may pile up, however, dictating the necessity of working evening or weekend hours in order to meet deadlines or solve problems. Travel may also be a prominent part of the job, and should be considered a definite possibility.

Because computer scientists and systems analysts spend long periods of time in front of a computer terminal typing on a keyboard, they are susceptible to eye strain, back discomfort, and hand and wrist problems.

TRAINING AND QUALIFICATIONS

College graduates are almost always sought for computer professional positions, and for some of the more complex jobs, persons with graduate degrees are preferred. Generally a computer scientist working in a research lab or academic institution will hold a Ph.D. or master's degree in computer science or engineering. Some computer scientists are able to gain sufficient experience for this type of position with only a bachelor's degree, but this is more difficult. Computer engineers generally have a bachelor's degree in computer engineering, electrical engineering, or mathematics. Computer designers need a minimum of a bachelor's degree in computer science or engineering. However, a master's degree is preferred.

Computer product design engineers are required to have a bachelor's degree in computer science or engineering. At one time, software designers were required to have a bachelor's or master's degree in computer science. But now experience may be given a considerable amount of weight also.

Software developers need to be flexible, organized, have strong interpersonal and technical skills, and have a high tolerance for failure and frustration. Professionals must be self-starters who can tackle problems head-on.

Software designers need to know program languages like COBOL, FORTRAN, ASCII or artificial intelligence or object-oriented languages like Prolog, LISP, and C++ as well as hardware and operating systems and other computer building blocks.

For database managers or administrators, a doctoral degree in computer science or advanced courses in computer programming may be required along with courses in business management and computer science. At lower positions, an associate's degree may be sufficient. Professionals in this field need to be skilled at managing databases and people.

The Institute for Certification of Computer Professionals offers the designation Certified Computing Professional (CCP) to those who have four years of experience and who pass a core examination plus exams in two specialty areas. Core exams are available in the following areas: microcomputers and networks, procedural programming, software engineering, systems programming, data resource management, management, business information systems, office information systems, systems development, communications, and systems security. The Quality Assurance Institute awards the designation Certified Quality Analyst (CQA) to those who meet education and experience requirements, pass an exam, and endorse a code of ethics. Neither designation is mandatory, but either may provide a job seeker a competitive advantage.

Computer support analysts may also need a bachelor's degree in a computer-related field, as well as significant experience working with computers, including programming skills.

The University of Illinois undergraduate catalog explains the value of a college or university education:

> Computer Science is a relatively young but extremely rich and diverse discipline. At one end of the spectrum, computer science may be viewed as the formal study of what can be computed and what resources are required for computation. At the other end of the spectrum, computer science may be seen as the application of hardware, software, and human resources to solve computational problems relating to society's and individuals' needs.
>
> A well-trained computer scientist requires a knowledge of both ends of this spectrum—and several points in between. The Computer Science Program in the Department of Electrical Engineering and Computer Science is intended to provide that broad background. Along with a strong theoretical component, the Computer Science Program places special emphasis on the development of applied skills in design, implementation, and validation of computer systems. In our experience, industry and graduate programs alike value—above all—people who can solve real problems, and who come prepared to use the tools of their trade.
>
> All students acquire a common background in the fundamental areas of computer science, computer systems, organization and architecture, algorithms and data structures, principles of software design, elements of the theory of computation, and operating systems. In addition, students obtain specialized backgrounds through the selection of five technical elective courses in computer science. Required and elective courses in the sciences and mathematics, along with additional courses in writing, humanities, social sciences, and the arts give students the opportunity to expand their horizons and to prepare for multidisciplinary careers.
>
> There are very few areas in modern society untouched by computer science. Computer science is present in everything from health care, telecommunications, and entertainment, to transportation, education, and defense. The result of this

diversity is that a computer scientist must be capable of working with people outside his or her field. In support of this, the Computer Science Program provides its students with a well-rounded education requiring significant course work outside the Department of Electrical Engineering and Computer Science, placing a strong emphasis on writing and communication skills.

The following course schedule, offered by the University of Illinois' Department of Electrical Engineering and Computer Science, offers a typical curriculum for computer science majors.

Typical Schedule for the Undergraduate Computer Science Major

FIRST YEAR
First Semester

Math 180—Calculus for Math, Engineering, and Science I

Science/engineering elective

Humanities/social sciences/arts elective

English 160—English Composition I

EECS 101—Introduction to Computing

Engr 100—Orientation

Second Semester

Math 181—Calculus for Math, Engineering, and Science II

Engl 161—English Composition II

Phys 141—General Physics I (Mechanics)

EECS 171—Introduction to Programming

SECOND YEAR
First Semester

Math 210—Calculus for Math, Engineering, and Science III

Humanities/social sciences/arts elective

EECS 260—Foundations of Computer Science

Phys 142—General Physics II (Electricity and Magnetism)

Free elective

Second Semester

EECS 265—Digital Systems

EECS 360—Data Structures and Algorithms

Required mathematics course

CEMM 200—Statics and Dynamics, or

ChE 201/ME 205—Thermodynamics, or

IE 201—Engineering Economics

Humanities/social sciences/arts elective

THIRD YEAR
First Semester

EECS 365—Computer Organization and Programming

EECS 370—Software Design

Required mathematics course

Humanities/social sciences/arts electives

Second Semester

EECS 361—Languages and Automata

EECS 366—Computer Architecture

EECS 371—Operating Systems Concepts and Design

Required mathematics course

Humanities/social sciences/arts electives

FOURTH YEAR
First Semester

EECS 375—Computer Ethics

EECS 460—Computer Algorithms

Technical electives

Humanities/social sciences/arts electives

Second Semester

Technical electives

Humanities/social sciences/arts electives

Qualifications for Systems Analysts

For a business environment, employers usually want systems analysts to have a background in business management or a closely related field. For scientifically oriented organizations, a background in the physical sciences, applied mathematics, or engineering is preferred. Many employers seek applicants who have a bachelor's degree in computer science, information science, computer information systems, or data processing. Regardless of the college major, employers look for people who are familiar with programming languages and have a broad knowledge of computer systems and technologies.

To achieve the title of systems analyst, one must have years of experience in data processing. This job experience is necessary for the analyst to fully comprehend the system being studied.

Systems analysts must be able to think logically, have good communication skills, and like working with people and ideas. They often deal with a number of tasks simultaneously. The ability to concentrate and pay close attention to detail also is important. Although systems analysts often work independently, they also work in teams on large projects. They must be able to communicate effectively with technical personnel, such as programmers and managers, as well as with other staff who may have no technical computer background.

Professionals with the title of systems analysts may be promoted to senior or lead systems analysts after gaining several years of experience. Those who show leadership abilities may advance to management positions, such as manager of information systems or chief information officer.

HELP WANTED

Systems Analyst

Our university is seeking a systems analyst. The successful candidate will provide system support, training, reporting, troubleshooting, and maintenance for mainframe, network, and PC systems and files for Enrollment Management at the school. In addition, responsibilities include working with vendors regarding interface and data transmissions. To qualify, you must possess a bachelor's degree with experience in programming and/or systems analysis. Excellent interpersonal and organizational skills required. Preferred candidates will have mainframe programming and/or analysis background and familiarity with CICS and COBOL. Expertise in network and/or PC operations and/or experience with student information systems a plus.

Many people develop advanced computer skills in other occupations in which they work extensively with computers and then transfer into computer occupations. For example, an accountant may become a systems analyst specializing in accounting systems development, or an individual may move into a systems analyst job after working as a computer programmer.

HELP WANTED

Systems Analyst

Join the team responsible for developing the latest in newspaper production automation. Join the systems development team which is looking for systems analysts with the following qualifications: BS/MS in Computer Science or a related field, experience with multiple operating systems—Sun Solaris, Windows 95, Mac Systems 7, proven programming skills in C, and exposure to databases (Oracle, Sybase, SQL).

In return, we offer all employees an excellent benefit and compensation package including medical and dental insurance, 401(k), tuition reimbursement, free life insurance, and much more. For immediate consideration, please forward your resume, including salary history.

EARNINGS

According to the *Occupational Outlook Handbook* prepared by the United States Department of Labor, the median annual earnings of computer systems analysts and scientists who work full time is about $44,000. The middle 50 percent earn between $34,100 and $55,000. The lowest 10 percent earn less than $25,100 and the highest 10 percent, more than $69,400.

Earnings for all computer scientists will vary according to the location, type of business, and size of the operation. Most positions offer paid holidays and vacations along with health insurance and sick leave.

According to Robert Half International Inc., starting salaries for systems analysts employed by large establishments that have more than 50 staff members range from $43,500 to $54,000. Salaries for those employed in small establishments range from $35,000 to $45,000.

In the federal government, the entrance salary for systems analysts who are recent college graduates with a bachelor's degree is about $18,700 a year; for those with a superior academic record, just over $23,000.

CAREER OUTLOOK

The *Occupational Outlook Handbook* predicts that computer scientists and systems analysts will be among the fastest-growing occupations through the year 2005. In addition, tens of thousands of job openings will result annually from the need to replace workers who move into managerial positions or other occupations or who leave the labor force.

The demand for computer scientists and engineers is expected to rise as organizations attempt to maximize the efficiency of their computer systems. There will continue to be a need for increasingly sophisticated technological innovation. Competition will place organizations under growing pressure to use technological advances in areas such as office and factory automation, telecommunications technology, and scientific research. As the complexity of these applications grows, more computer scientists and systems analysts will be needed to design, develop, and implement the new technology.

As more computing power is made available to the individual user, more computer scientists and systems analysts will be required to provide support. As users develop more sophisticated knowledge of computers, they become more aware of the machine's potential and better able to suggest how computers could be used to increase their own productivity and that of the organization. Increasingly, users are able to design and implement more of their own applications and programs. As technology continues to advance, computer scientists and systems analysts will continue to need to upgrade their levels of skill and technical expertise, and their ability to interact with users will increase in importance.

The demand for "networking" to facilitate the sharing of information will be a major factor in the rising demand for systems analysts. Falling prices of computer hardware and software should continue to induce more small businesses to computerize their operations, further stimulating demand for these workers. In order to maintain a competitive edge and operate more cost effectively, firms will continue to demand computer professionals who are knowledgeable about the latest technologies and able to apply them to meet the needs of businesses. A greater emphasis on problem-solving, analysis, and client/server environments will also contribute to the growing demand for systems analysts.

STRATEGY FOR FINDING THE JOBS

Individuals with an advanced degree in computer science should enjoy very favorable employment prospects because employers are demanding a higher level of technical expertise. College graduates with a bachelor's degree in computer science, computer engineering, information science, or information systems should experience good prospects for employment. College graduates with noncomputer science majors who have had courses in computer programming, systems analysis, and other data processing areas, as well as training or experience in an applied field, may also be able to find jobs as computer professionals. Those who are familiar with CASE tools, object-oriented and client/server programming, and multimedia technology will have an even greater advantage, as will individuals with significant networking, database, and systems experience.

Working through campus employment services is still the best place for graduates to begin to seek job positions. Often, potential employers come to campuses to look for and interview potential candidates. Technical job fairs (both on and off campus) are also possibilities for potential employment. Want ads (similar to those included in this book) may be found in any newspaper—particularly the Sunday edition. Since virtually any company may avail itself of the services of computer scientists, there is a potential to land a job almost anywhere. Networking techniques are very important as are other avenues such as joining professional associations, volunteering to help in a local, school, or community project, and seeking the aid of mentors.

PROFESSIONAL ASSOCIATIONS

American Electronics Association
5201 Great America Parkway, Suite 520
Santa Clara, CA 95054

American Society for Information Sciences (ASIS)
8720 Georgia Avenue
Silver Spring, MD 20910

Association for Computing Machinery
11 West 42nd Street
New York, NY 10036

Association for Women in Computing
P.O. Box 21100
St. Paul, MN 55123

Association of Computer Professionals
230 Park Avenue
New York, New York 10169

Interactive Multimedia Association
48 Maryland Avenue, Suite 202
Annapolis, MD 21401

Institute for the Certification of Computing Professionals
2200 East Devon Avenue, Suite 268
Des Plaines, IL 60018

Networking Professionals Association
151 East 1700 South
Provo, UT 84606

Quality Assurance Institute
7575 Phillips Boulevard, Suite 350
Orlando, FL 32819

Semiconductor Industry Association
181 Metro Drive, Suite 450
San Jose, CA 95110

Software Forum
P.O. Box 61031
Palo Alto, CA 94306

MEET RON BURRIS

Ron Burris earned an associate in arts degree through Allan Hancock College; an associate in science degree through the Ground Wire Communications Technology program of the Community College of the Air Force, and also attended the computer programming technical school in Biloxi, Mississippi, in addition to some classes at San Diego State College. He has extensive experience in hardware and software programs, software development, systems analysis network design, end-user support and education, project planning, accounting and management, technical and proposal writing, retail and consulting business operations, management and telephone plant installation, maintenance operations, and management. He has served as a software engineer, technical writer, programmer/analyst, and consultant and is currently employed by Medical Matrix, Inc., in Fort Worth, Texas, as a software engineer.

"I began as a hobbyist in 1975," says Burris. "Subsequently, I entered the computer field professionally in 1978, when I started writing articles for *Kilobaud* magazine (the second national microcomputer magazine—

continued

continued

Byte was first). I've always been technically inclined," he says, "building radios, electronic test equipment, etc., since I was in grammar school.

"After private contract consulting for several years, I took a job designing and programming software for my present employer, a pharmaceutical claims processor. It's a small company (35 employees), with four in the computer services department. The atmosphere is fairly casual, though the pace is hectic. We're maintaining an inadequately written software system while designing, building, and implementing replacement software. Due to constantly changing requirements from and for our clients, we do a lot of 'batch and patch' programming to keep the revenue flowing while we work toward an elegant solution. The hours per week vary from about 30 to about 50, depending on what's going on.

"I like the autonomy of this position," Burris says. "My supervisor allows me the flexibility to get the job done on my terms, as long as it's done well. My least favorite thing is being interrupted in my work to fix someone else's computer—usually simple stuff they could do themselves. On the other hand, I am paid well, receive a good benefits package, and work close to home. On the downside is the fact that prior management bought overly cheap equipment and hired programmers who didn't believe in using database software to maintain databases, which makes the code tracing to fix a simple problem a nightmare.

"I would advise others to live long and prosper—keep up on current technology, and avoid following the fads."

MEET STEVE PFLUG

Steve Pflug is Network Administrator for Arthur Andersen in Kansas City, Missouri. He attended DeVry Technical Institute in Kansas City and received a bachelor of arts degree in telecommunications management. His previous experience includes PC support and networking.

"I entered the computer field via the Air Force," Pflug says. "As a network administrator, 75 percent of a typical day is spent fielding service requests, mainly printer-related problems. I spend most of the remaining 25 percent dealing with user problems. I also take some time to customize service reports and forms for people. Somehow every day, I also sandwich in reviewing and reading about the software the company uses. I feel that it's important to keep up with the latest technology.

continued

continued

"Our work atmosphere is very relaxed and laid back," he says. "I usually work an average of 50 hours per week including some evenings and weekends. The hectic time is during implementation of new software and upgrades.

"In order to succeed in a position such as this, you need minor programming skills; networking and topography background; good knowledge of computers; networks; troubleshooting; software programs; databases; spreadsheets; data processing; patience; good research and development skills; a background in finance; and project management skills.

"The best thing about this position is that it has provided a chance for me to explore and educate myself in many new areas and also given me the foundation that should provide an opportunity to become a consultant (in about four or five years). I also like the upgrading and training people on the new software which is part of the job.

"What I like the least is the monotony at times when projects are not happening. I hate having to look for projects to do. It is also difficult to initiate new projects when there are constant worries about the client's financial situation. This is frustrating because then the company cannot keep current with the new technological advances. But we do our best.

"I would advise others to make sure you get a good education. Be well-rounded in computer knowledge. I'd also suggest that you do an internship while you are still in school."

MEET TIM LEE

Tim Lee is a Network Consultant/LAN Administrator for Anderson Consulting in Lincoln, Nebraska. He earned a bachelor of science degree in economics from Kansas State University in Manhattan, Kansas, and an M.B.A. from Kansas State University in Kansas City, Missouri.

"While working in mutual fund processing, I developed computer system knowledge that led to me taking this job. Before this, I hadn't worked in the field of computers, although they have always interested me," says Lee.

"About half of my day is spent in day-to-day operations management, implementing changes to the system, finding solutions to ongoing problems. I spend about 30 percent of the day on the phone with clients, helping them solve their computer problems. The other 20 percent is spent documenting what I've done that day to help clients.

continued

continued

"In order to serve in this position, you need to have good problem-solving skills, PC and network experience, experience in customer service/relationship building, organizational skills, networking skills, and the ability to work in a team setting.

"Our company maintains an open-door policy. We tend to work at the client's site, so it's not exactly a casual setting. Our most hectic times are when the computer goes down, or when new programs are being implemented. I work an average of 40 to 50 hours per week, some evenings.

"What I like best about this job is having the freedom to do what is best for the client. Management really encourages us to be creative with our ideas. We work very much in a team setting—which is nice. My boss is very good at hands-off management style. He trusts me to do what is best for the client. There is a strong entrepreneurial spirit here. I dislike working under the constraints of a state budget, as funds are limited, but on the positive side, it presents challenges in offering the customer the most for the money that is available.

"I'd advise prospective candidates to learn as much as you can about computer software and systems. It's important to develop great problem-solving and customer relationship skills. You have to be a people person. Gain experience as you study. Always keep in mind that your experience will help you in the future."

MEET BRIAN KILLEN

Brian Killen earned a bachelor of science degree in computer science from Kansas State University in Manhattan, Kansas. He has enhanced his expertise by attending numerous seminars—anything to do with software engineering development.

"I became interested in computers while in high school," he reveals. "And during college I served in an internship with a computer services organization. I have always wanted to develop products that help people communicate with each other.

"Our work atmosphere is extremely casual. I work in an office where the set hours are Monday through Friday from 8:30 A.M. until 5 P.M. However, the truth is that I usually work 50 to 60 hours per week. During crunch time it can be 70 hours per week. It's a very intense job, definitely not low-key.

"Our days are influenced by the projects we are working on at the time," he says, "and the projects run on one- to two-year cycles. In

continued

continued

the beginning of a project, there is a lot of thinking, designing, and talking to customers. The latter half of a project is spent sitting at the keyboard and writing code all day. (I would say 50 percent of the project is spent writing code.) It is the last five months of a project that are the busiest and most stressful.

"The staff convenes weekly meetings via teleconference as some working on the projects are in California and India.

"What I like best is creating the products for people to use. What I like least is the turnaround time for a product. It takes two years to see end results—to feel the full gratification of the job.

"In order to serve in this position effectively, you need experience in designing user interfaces, software engineering skills, programming skills—networking, protocol development, C++ language—patience, the ability to work in a team setting, the ability to keep the customer in mind, the ability to work well with a diverse group of people, good communication and interpersonal skills, attention to detail, stamina to work on a project for years, persistence, and insight into where the industry is going.

"You really have to like this kind of work to do this job because it's quite demanding. Long, difficult, stressful hours are fairly common. I'd advise others to get as much experience as early as possible because this isn't a job you really come to understand in college. It's a job you learn by doing. Once you experience the doing, you'll be able to determine if this is something that you truly want to make your life's work."

CHAPTER ELEVEN

PATH 2: MANAGEMENT ANALYSTS AND CONSULTANTS

"One of the most feared expressions in modern times is 'The computer is down.'"

—Norman Augustine

HELP WANTED

Consultant

Selected candidates will: plan, analyze, and recommend cost-effective architectures, infrastructures, and standards that adapt to changing business needs, reduce cycle time, and leverage bottom-line results; develop strategy and direction for client/server infrastructure within a large multisite, multiplatform environment; implement new client/server architecture and release phases of client/server initiates. Qualified candidates should possess: 3.5+ years proven experience with large-scale client/server systems as well as experience with requirements analysis data and process modeling, logical/physical design and knowledge of structure methodologies and project planning.

DEFINITION OF THE CAREER PATH

Management Analyst or Consultant

The career called management consulting is a relatively new occupation, born in the 1960s as a result of the growth of the management sciences as a valid academic course of study. Business schools and economics departments across the nation promoted this growth through their literature on the subject of management organization and analysis of work and company efficiency. They began collecting and distributing data on productivity and capacity of organizations, giving companies a greater understanding of the forces affecting them. The 1970s saw the development of small consulting firms with specific areas of expertise, and the 1980s saw the birth of the management consultant generalist who applied general principles of management to individual companies and then offered recommendations.

Management analysts and consultants are problem solvers who piece together puzzles and apply theory to real life in order to suggest solutions to management problems. They are experts at setting up and using computer systems. Companies who wish to reach optimum levels of efficiency and profitability hire management consultants to identify causes and recommend solutions to situations and practices. For example, a rapidly growing small company may need help in designing a better system of control over inventories and expenses, or an established manufacturing company may need assistance in relocating to another state, or a large company may want to reorganize after acquiring a new division. These are just a few of the many organizational problems that management analysts (as they are called in government agencies) and management consultants (as business firms refer to them) help solve.

Consultants' tasks may be sharply defined, such as analyzing the shipping function and streamlining procedures, or broadly defined, such as reorganizing a multinational corporation to take advantage of the synergies that developed when it acquired new businesses.

The work of management analysts and consultants varies by client or employer and from project to project. For example, some projects require a team of consultants, each specializing in one area; at other times, consultants will work independently of each other with the client's managers.

Upon getting an assignment or contract, consultants and analysts try to define the nature and extent of the problem. During this phase of the job, they may analyze data such as annual revenues, employment, or expenditures. Then they interview managers and employees and observe the operations of the organizational unit.

Next, they use their knowledge of management systems and their expertise in a particular area to develop solutions to the problem. In the course of preparing their recommendations, they must take into account the general nature of the business, the relationship the firm has with others in that industry, and the firm's internal organization and culture, as well as information gained through data collection and analysis.

Once they have decided on a course of action, consultants usually report their findings and recommendations to the client, often in writing. In addition, they generally make oral presentations regarding their findings. For some projects, this is all that is required; for others, consultants may assist in the implementation of their suggestions.

Management analysts in government agencies use the same skills as their private-sector colleagues in advising managers in government on many types of issues, most of which are similar to the problems faced by private firms. For example, if an agency is planning to purchase personal computers, it first must determine which type to buy, given its budget and data processing needs. Management analysts would assess the various types of machines available (by price range) and determine which best meets the department's needs.

HELP WANTED

Consultants Who Can Walk on Water

Actually, our standards are slightly lower than that. But if your consulting skills are truly outstanding, then give us a call and tell us about yourself. If you have skills in any of the following areas, we'll walk on water to keep you busy with consulting assignments.

- Informix—4GL

- IEF—Composer

- MS Access, Crystal Reports

If you'd rather be making money than looking for assignments, give us a call. Even if you aren't immediately available—or if you've got miraculous skills not listed—get in touch today!

JOB TITLES

Computer consultants

Management analysts

Management consultants

HELP WANTED

Consultant
Needed for installation, training, and implementing systems.
Software applications include associations, small manufacturing,
and distribution. Applicants should have good communication skills
as well as PC Windows skills.

POSSIBLE EMPLOYERS

Management consultants may be hired to do whatever helps a client's bottom line. Clients range from companies that are on the cutting edge of their industries and want help in staying ahead to companies who are in trouble and need help staying afloat.

Both public and private organizations use consultants. Some don't have the internal resources needed to handle a project; others need a consultant's expertise to determine what resources will be required, and what problems may be encountered, if they pursue a particular course of action. Still others want to get outside help on how to resolve organizational problems that have already been identified or to avoid troublesome problems that could arise.

Firms providing consulting services range in size from solo practitioners to large international organizations employing thousands of consultants. Some firms specialize by industry, while others specialize by type of business function, such as human resources or information systems. In government, management analysts tend to specialize by type of agency. Consulting services usually are provided on a contractual basis whereby a company solicits proposals from a number of consulting firms specializing in the area in which it needs assistance. These proposals include the estimated cost and scope of the project, staffing requirements, references from a number of previous clients, and the deadline. The company then selects the proposal that best meets its needs.

Many management consulting firms work for federal, state, and local governments. The majority of those working for the federal government are found in the Department of Defense.

Management analysts and consultants are found throughout the country, but employment is concentrated in large metropolitan areas.

RELATED OCCUPATIONS

Management analysts and consultants collect, review, and analyze data; make recommendations; and assist in the implementation of their ideas. Other careers that utilize similar skills are:

Computer systems analyst	Operations research analyst
Economist	Physical scientist
Financial analyst	Researcher
Investment banker	Social scientist
Life scientist	Sociologist
Manager	Urban planner

WORKING CONDITIONS

Management analysts and consultants usually divide their time between their offices and their client's site. Although much of their time is spent indoors in clean, well-lighted offices, they may have to visit a client's production facility where conditions may not be so favorable.

Meetings are common and usually serve as forums for brainstorming, discussing new approaches to tackling a problem, and sharing work with other case team members or with the client.

Typically, analysts and consultants work at least 40 hours a week, although the figure may certainly vary. Travel, perhaps frequently, may also be required. Overtime is common, especially when project deadlines are near.

Self-employed consultants can set their workloads and hours and work at home. On the other hand, their livelihoods depend on their ability to maintain and expand their client bases. Salaried consultants also must favorably impress potential clients to get and keep clients for their companies.

Computer consultants usually work independently on a contract basis. Some consultants are employed by consulting firms. The hours will vary as do the lengths of contracts. They may be hourly or monthly or for very extended periods of time.

TRAINING AND QUALIFICATIONS

No specific academic requirements exist for management analysts and consultants, but nearly all employers require at least a college degree in computer science or a related field such as business, economics, data processing, statistics, mathematics, or logic.

Educational requirements for entry-level jobs in this field vary widely, but there is an increasing emphasis on scientific and technological applications at the undergraduate level. Employers in private industry generally seek individuals with a master's degree in business administration or a related discipline. Individuals hired straight out of school with only a bachelor's degree are generally hired as research associates and will find it difficult to advance up the career ladder unless they return to school for an advanced degree.

Most government agencies hire people with a bachelor's degree and no work experience as entry-level management analysts, and often pay for graduate classes in management analysis.

In large consulting firms, beginners are usually assigned research work for consulting teams. (Most major employers run their own programs to train junior consultants in accounting, internal policy, research techniques, and how to work as part of a hard-working team.) The team is responsible for the entire project and each consultant is assigned to a particular area. As consultants gain experience, they may be assigned to work on one specific project full time, taking on more responsibility and managing their own hours. At the senior level, consultants may supervise entry-level workers and become increasingly involved in seeking out new business. Those with exceptional skills may eventually become partners or principals in the firm. Others with entrepreneurial ambition may open their own firms. At all levels, continuing education is recommended through attending seminars, classes, and conferences.

Many fields of study provide a suitable educational background for this occupation because of the diversity of problem areas addressed by management analysts and consultants. These include most areas of business and management, as well as computer and information sciences and engineering.

Candidates need a background in one or two programming languages and knowledge of a hardware platform (IBM or its clones). Consultants with broader skills know several different programming languages and are familiar with computer-aided software engineering (CASE) technology, and can not only develop new information systems but can integrate new components with old ones. Experts in database management systems, artificial intelligence, technology planning, multilevel database security, and other specific areas are in the stratosphere of consulting.

To be successful, consultants must be exceptional both analytically and interpersonally. Analytically, they should possess superior problem-solving skills, linear logical thinking, and strong presentation development skills. They also need to be very effective listeners and be able to clearly, concisely, and persuasively communicate their findings to a wide range of people with differing backgrounds and needs.

A high percentage of management consultants are self-employed, partly because business start-up costs are low. Self-employed consultants also can share office space, administrative help, and other resources with other self-employed consultants or small consulting firms, thus reducing overhead costs. Many such firms fail, however, because of an inability to acquire and maintain a profitable client base.

The Institute of Management Consultants (a division of the Council of Consulting Organizations, Inc.) offers the Certified Management Consultant (CMC) designation to those who pass an examination and meet minimum levels of education and experience. Certification is not mandatory for management consultants to practice, but it may give a job seeker a competitive advantage.

HELP WANTED

Consultants
We need the best!

Our consulting division needs contractors with the following specifications:

SQL developer

Microsoft CNE

Relational DBA

Java, Active-X

Please state availability and rate.

EARNINGS

Salaries for management analysts and consultants vary widely by experience, education, and employer. The *Occupational Outlook Handbook* published by the United States Department of Labor reports that full-time salaried workers have median annual earnings of about $41,300. The middle 50 percent earn between $30,000 and $53,900.

According to the Association of Management Consulting Firms (AMCF), earnings, including bonuses and/or profit sharing for research associates in AMCF member firms average $30,400; for entry-level consultants, $41,800; for management consultants, $58,300; for senior consultants, $89,200; for junior partners, $120,100; and for senior partners, $194,000.

Typical benefits for salaried analysts and consultants include health and life insurance, a retirement plan, vacation and sick leave, profit sharing, and bonuses for outstanding work. In addition, all travel expenses usually are reimbursed by the employer. Self-employed consultants usually have to maintain their own offices and provide their own benefits.

HELP WANTED

Consulting Opportunities

Our Consulting Inc. seeks qualified professionals for local consulting assignments. Outstanding rewards, flexible hours, and long-term engagements await those who wish to advance their career with us. Experience with PeopleSoft software of Year 2000 project a plus. Fax resume.

CAREER OUTLOOK

This is a growing profession—faster than average through 2005 since industry and government will increasingly look to these professions. However, competition for these positions will continue to be intense. Aspiring consultants should prepare for this challenge by achieving strong academic records, gaining work experience that demonstrates competence and maturity, and becoming knowledgeable about accounting and financial issues.

Growth is expected in large consulting firms, but also in small consulting firms whose consultants will specialize in specific areas of expertise. Because many small consulting firms fail each year due to lack of managerial expertise and clients, those interested in opening their own firms must have good organizational and marketing skills, plus several years of consulting experience.

Increased competition has forced American industry to take a closer look at its operations. As international and domestic markets become more competitive, firms must use what resources they have more efficiently. Management consultants are being increasingly relied upon to help reduce costs, streamline operations, and develop marketing strategies. As businesses downsize and eliminate needed functions as well as permanent staff, consultants will be used to perform those functions that were previously handled internally. Businesses attempting to expand, particularly into world markets, frequently need the skills of management consultants to help with organizational, administrative, and other issues. Continuing changes in the business environment also are expected to lead to a demand for management consultants. Firms will use consultants to incorporate new technologies, to cope with more numerous and complex government regulations, and to adapt to a changing labor force. As businesses rely more on technology, there are increasing roles for consultants with a technical background, such as engineering or biotechnology, particularly when combined with an M.B.A.

Federal, state, and local agencies also are expected to expand their use of management analysts. In the era of budget deficits, analysts' skills at identifying problems and implementing cost-reduction measures are expected to become increasingly important. However, because almost one-half of the management analysts employed by the federal government work for the Department of Defense, federal employment growth will increase slowly because of cutbacks in the nation's defense budget.

Despite projected rapid employment growth, competition for jobs as management consultants is expected to be keen in the private sector. Because management consultants can come from such diverse educational backgrounds, the pool of applicants from which employers hire is quite large. Additionally, the independent and challenging nature of the work combined with high earnings potential make this occupation attractive to many. Job opportunities are expected to be best for those with a graduate degree and some industry expertise.

PROFESSIONAL ASSOCIATIONS

American Management Association
135 West 50th Street
New York, NY 10020

Association of Management Consulting Firms
521 Fifth Avenue, 35th Floor
New York, NY 10175

Council of Consultant Organizations
521 Fifth Avenue, 35th Floor
New York, NY 10175

Independent Computer Consultants Association
933 Gardenview Office Parkway
St. Louis, MO 63141

National Association of Computer Consulting Businesses
1250 Connecticut Avenue, NW, Suite 700
Washington, DC 20036

Office of Personnel Management
1900 E Street, NW
Washington, DC 20415

MEET JEFFREY SKIPPEN

Jeffrey Skippen earned a bachelor of science degree (with honors) in computer studies/geography from Trent University in Peterborough, Ontario, Canada.

continued

continued

He has attained the status of Novell Master CNE, and Microsoft Certified Professional and serves as a senior network management consultant for a governmental agency.

"I started as a computing services laboratory monitor at Trent University in 1989," he explains. "Then I became a LAN administrator for the Department of Justice, first as a summer student, then as a full-time government employee and then two additional years as a consultant. For the past two years I have been acting as the senior network management consultant for a major government department.

"The importance of the computer industry led me to focus on a combined major of geography and computer studies," explains Skippen. "Geography had been my primary interest, but it was becoming obvious to me that computer technology would have a major impact on the future job market. I became a LAN administrator for several summer terms while at school. This eventually led me to choose a career as a network specialist. I always enjoyed tinkering with computers, which were easier for me to understand than other, less defined disciplines such as geography, English, social sciences, etc. Computers either worked, or they didn't work. They didn't argue with you, or make you try to see their point of view. I found the problems presented by computer technology easier to solve than those presented by social and political environments. Best of all, others were amazed when you could fix things that they couldn't possibly understand (no matter how easy it was for you to do so).

"Today my job can be near boring—to absolutely terrifying. In my earlier days I was assigned to a project for a cement-mixing company. One of their networked PCs ran an application that mixed the water with the cement and the company was totally dependent on it. I was doing some work on the computer that ran the mixing application and something went wrong and the computer would not function properly. (Backups and documentation were not concepts this company was familiar with at the time.) After about a half hour of down time, I looked out from the window in the cement silo to see about ten cement trucks lined up waiting to get their loads. All I could think of at the time was that if I didn't get this system running soon, they would probably be making me a special pair of swimming shoes. Needless to say, I got the system running again and everyone was happy (especially me).

"Every job is a new one with a new combination of variables—the learning process is constant and you never know what situation you are going to face next. Technology changes daily—you cannot possibly keep up-to-date with every change. After a while you develop your own methodology of

continued

continued

solving problems—and if it is a good, sound methodology, chances are
you are going to be successful with it throughout your career. But you
must always have a methodology. If you leap before you look, you will
eventually get yourself into trouble. If you use a sound methodology to
solve problems, and you work to perfect it, you will usually come off
looking like a hero. And that is the feeling that makes this industry
worthwhile—a feeling of self-value and knowing that your contributions made the difference between delight and disaster.

"My hours vary depending on the projects. On the maintenance and
installation side of things, you should get used to working weekends and
evenings. If you are in day-to-day operations, you will probably work
regular hours. Most of us end up doing a combination of these hours
and wearing a pocket pager.

"The best part of this job is when I am able to solve complicated
problems that made a difference to the client. Many times your efforts
will go unnoticed, but eventually you will find the needle in the haystack when someone important is watching.

"Downsides are the times spent in between finding the needle in the
haystack. I have to admit I have come close to the borderline of insanity
in certain situations. In one situation an entire company was down for
several days while I was trying to find out what was wrong with their
system. I replaced every piece of hardware from A to Z piece by piece—
and it still failed. The problem ended up being the client's power supply, but by the time we figured that out I was ready to leave and get into
aluminum siding or the clergy.

"A home computer is an essential tool if you are going into this industry.
It is your toolbox and your connection to the world—you must have one!

"Computers don't make mistakes—people do! But since people are sign-
ing your paychecks, you should be as kind and understanding to them as
possible. There is a lot of user frustration out there, and you will always be
in the line of fire when you come to fix a problem. Never assume the client
has any knowledge, but always talk to the client as though they do."

MEET TOM TESKA

Tom Teska earned a bachelor of science degree in computer science from
the University of Wisconsin in Madison, Wisconsin.

He has served as a consultant since 1980 and a Certified Network
Engineer since 1991. He also received training on Netware 4.x Administration and design and took a class on teaching Novell courses.

continued

continued

"My father opened a ComputerLand store in 1980," says Teska. "When we brought the computers in for his original stock, I started using them. I discovered that I loved working on them and making them do things that no one else could do. From there, I went to helping people use them better. The consulting work lets me do this and work on computers—the best of both worlds.

"Over the years, my job has changed many times. When I worked in the commercial sector, I operated at a very high pace. My work with ComputerLand and Entre stores had me supporting upwards of 1,000 companies with tens of thousands of people. I was typically working 60 to 70 hours a week for months on end.

"I am now employed by a long-term contract consulting firm and the pace is much slower. I report to only one client supporting less than 10,000 people and now work a standard 40-hour week. When I was assigned to commercial stores, there was no such thing as a typical day. That was actually one of the things I liked about it. I supported people in many different industries as well as our internal staff. One day I'd be working with bankers and the next day I'd be helping teachers in an elementary school. Now that I support only one company, I do have typical days. I work in a cubicle with several other support people. We install and support applications and maintain the large WAN that is installed here. I also work on the second-level help desk, which means that I get the problem calls that the first-level people can't solve.

"The thing I like most about being a consultant/support person is being able to get people's PCs to do things that no one else can do. People call me when they've got a problem that they haven't been able to solve and I fix it for them. It makes me feel good to help them like that, and I enjoy the thanks I get from the users in those situations. I also look forward to the actual work with the computers. I have fun while I'm working!

"When I worked in the commercial end of this field, I also got to work with cutting-edge technology. It was really enjoyable to work on new systems that no one had tried before. I find it particularly pleasurable to learn new things.

"My least favorite aspect of this business is having to solve the same problems over and over. That can be frustrating because I know I just solved this problem for someone else three weeks ago but I can't remember exactly how, so I have to do all the same work again. Secondly, once you've got that memorized and are called upon to fix

continued

continued

the same problem, you don't learn anything new. Another minor an-
noyance is that every once in a while I run into a customer who isn't
satisfied, no matter what I do. Luckily, this doesn't happen very often. Most of the time, people are very appreciative of my knowledge
and my efforts.

"I feel that the most important thing about being a consultant is
to keep learning. I think it's my job to know more about PCs and
networks and software than my customers. Thus, I constantly seek
out new information through reading and enrolling in classes in order to be aware of the new strategies and technologies that come to
light virtually every day in this ever-changing field."

CHAPTER TWELVE

PATH 3: OPERATIONS RESEARCH ANALYSTS

"We live in a time when automation is ushering in a second industrial revolution."

—Adlai Stevenson

HELP WANTED

Operations Research Analyst
Information Services Group

We are in need of an Operations Research Analyst who will be responsible for understanding, evaluating, and extending the algorithmic components of an Airline Yield Management True Origin and Destination Application.

The successful candidate will have a background in Operations Research with at least two years experience. A Bachelor's Degree in Operations Research is required, with a Master's strongly preferred. Experience in airlines or revenue management is desirable, but not required. Strong communications skills are required, both written and verbal. The successful candidate will also bring some or all of the following: C/C++ programming experience; Object Oriented design experience—Rational-Rose preferred; RDBMS experience—Oracle preferred; UNIX; Client Server experience—Tuxedo preferred; Windows NT and GUI development skills. We offer a competitive salary and professional opportunity and growth.

Definition of the Career Path

Operations Research Analyst

If you're the one in your group who has always been delighted by problem-solving via math word problems, operational research analysis might be just the career for you! Acting in the capacity of industry problem solvers, operations research analysts (also called management science analysts) use their computer expertise along with their scientific, mathematical, and analytical methods to promote the smooth operations of companies.

Depending on your area of specialization—in industry, government, or international relations—you might be asked to help answer complex questions like: How can a dress manufacturer lay out its patterns to minimize wasted material? How often should the sales force of a frozen yogurt company call on its customers? How many elevators should be installed in a new office building to cut waiting time? What's the most efficient method for routing a long-distance telephone call?

HELP WANTED

Operations Research Analyst

Our consulting company is one of the world's premier management and technology consultancies. We work with many of the largest and most successful organizations to develop integrated solutions that transform their enterprises. By understanding the key components that drive an organization—Strategy, Technology, Business Processes, and People—we have established an unrivaled track record of developing tangible results and competitive advantage to our clients.

This position requires a minimum of two years experience in the following:

Client/Server, UNIX, Oracle

Windows 95 or NT

MIMI, Manugistics, and AION software

Systems Analysis and Design Implementation

Planning and Scheduling/Supply Chain Experience

continued

---

continued

Responsibilities include:

Participation in development of application architecture for steel in planning and scheduling

Create functional specifications specific to planning and scheduling optimization, algorithmic, and heuristic techniques

Provide production support for a specific application or group of applications.

Salary commensurate with skills and experience. Qualified candidates should send a resume and salary history.

Operations research and management science are two terms that are pretty much used interchangeably to describe the same field (which is also sometimes called decision technology). Basically, operations research is a scientific approach to analyzing problems and making decisions. It uses mathematics and mathematical modeling on computers to forecast the implications of various choices and zero in on the best alternatives.

Developed during World War II, operations research helped take the guesswork out of deploying radar, searching for enemy submarines, getting supplies where they were most needed, and the like. And following the war, numerous peacetime applications emerged.

Manufacturers used operations research to make products more efficiently, schedule equipment maintenance, and control inventory and distribution. Success in these areas led to expansion into strategic and financial planning and into such diverse areas as criminal justice, education, meteorology, and communications.

Operations analysts always begin by learning everything they can about the problem at hand. In order to accomplish this, they talk with people involved in all aspects of it, soliciting their varying perspectives and needs and their input into the solution. They examine available data, separating that which is truly relevant from that which is not. And they focus on practical, workable results, making sure what they propose is not just a theoretically appealing model, but one that will function effectively in the real world.

At this point the operations research analysts present their reports to management along with recommendations based upon their findings. Once there is acceptance of the analyst's work, all parties work together for its implementation.

Operations research analysts use computers extensively in their work. They are typically highly proficient in database management, programming, and in the development and use of sophisticated software programs. Most of the models built by operations research analysts are so complicated that only a computer can solve them efficiently.

The type of problem they usually handle varies by industry. For example, an analyst for an airline would coordinate flight and maintenance scheduling, passenger-level estimates, and fuel consumption to produce a schedule that optimizes all of these factors to ensure safety and produce the most profits. An analyst employed by a hospital would concentrate on a different set of problems—scheduling admissions, managing patient flow, assigning shifts, monitoring use of pharmacy and laboratory services, or forecasting demand for new hospital services.

The role of the operations research analyst varies according to the structure and management philosophy of the firm. Some centralize operations research in one department; others disperse operations research personnel throughout all divisions. Some operations research analysts specialize in one type of application; others are generalists.

Efficiently running a complex organization or operation such as a large manufacturing plant, an airline, or a military deployment requires the precise coordination of materials, machines, and people. Operations research analysts help organizations coordinate and operate in the most efficient manner by applying scientific methods and mathematical principles to organizational problems. Managers can then evaluate alternatives and choose the course of action that best meets the organizational goals.

The degree of supervision varies by organizational structure and experience. In some organizations, analysts have a great deal of professional autonomy, while in others, analysts are more closely supervised. Operations research analysts work closely with senior managers, who have a wide variety of support needs. Analysts must adapt their work to reflect these requirements.

JOB TITLES

Operations research analyst

POSSIBLE EMPLOYERS

In the United States and around the world, there are a wide variety of job openings in both the public and private sectors. Operations research analysts are employed in most industries. Many large manufacturers, retail chains, and service organizations maintain an in-house staff, ranging in size from one or two operations researchers to a full department. Major employers include computer and data processing services, commercial banks and savings institutions, insurance carriers, telecommunication companies, engineering and management services firms, manufacturers of transportation equipment, and air carriers. American Airlines, AT&T, Citicorp, Merrill Lynch, American Express, and General Motors are just a few examples of firms that employ sizable numbers.

The largest employer is the United States government—specifically the Departments of Labor, Commerce, Housing and Urban Development, Transportation, Defense, and Health and Human Services, as well as the Government Accounting Office and Congressional Budget Office. All branches of the armed services also work with both civilian and military operations researchers. (In addition, many operations research analysts who work in private industry perform work directly or indirectly related to national defense.) And an increasing number of state and local jurisdictions are hiring both staffers and consultants, as are the governments of other countries.

About two out of ten analysts work for management, research, public relations, and testing agencies that do operations research.

Related Occupations

Operations research analysts apply mathematical principles to large, complicated problems. Workers in other occupations that stress quantitative analysis include computer scientists, engineers, mathematicians, statisticians, and economists. Operations research is closely allied to managerial occupations in that its goal is improved organizational efficiency.

Working Conditions

Operations research analysts generally work regular hours in an office environment. Because they work on projects that are of immediate interest to management, analysts often are under pressure to meet deadlines and often work more than a 40-hour week.

Training and Qualifications

Companies expect that individuals who seek employment have attained at least an undergraduate degree in the computer field or a related area. In fact, employers strongly prefer applicants with at least a master's degree in operations research or management science, or other quantitative disciplines. Over 150 colleges and universities in the United States and abroad offer degree programs or courses in operations research and closely allied fields.

Employers will expect that candidates have a solid grounding in statistics, probability, calculus, linear algebra, other advanced mathematics, and economics. Because the field relies so heavily on computers, companies will assume you have an understanding of how computers work and how to program them. You will also need a familiarity with software such as AMPL, LINDO, CPLEX, and SAS, along with an interest in using it as a decision tool. Since research is interdisciplinary, often drawing solutions from engineering, logic, psychology, and other social and political sciences, a well-rounded scientific background proves useful. Exceptional interpersonal and communications skills will serve you well as will a high degree of initiative, energy, and maturity. You will be expected to perform well on your own or as a member of a team.

Beginning analysts usually do routine work under the supervision of more experienced analysts. As they gain knowledge and experience, they are assigned more complex tasks, with greater autonomy to design models and solve problems. Operations research analysts advance by assuming positions as technical specialists or supervisors. The skills acquired by operations research analysts are useful for higher-level management jobs, and experienced analysts may leave the field altogether to assume nontechnical managerial or administrative positions.

Employers often sponsor skill improvement training for experienced workers, helping them keep up with new developments in operations research techniques as well as advances in computer science. Some analysts attend advanced university classes on these subjects at their employer's expense.

EARNINGS

According to recruiters and national operations research associations, operations research analysts with a master's degree generally earn starting salaries of about $36,000 to $45,000 a year. Experienced operations research analysts earn about $50,000 to $60,000 a year. Top salaries exceed $90,000.

The average annual salary for operations research analysts in the federal government in nonsupervisory, supervisory, and managerial positions is $62,450.

CAREER OUTLOOK
···························

Organizations are increasingly using operations research and management science techniques to improve productivity and quality and to reduce costs. This reflects growing acceptance of a systematic approach to decision-making by top managers. This trend is expected to continue and should greatly stimulate demand for these workers in the years ahead.

Those seeking employment as operations research or management science analysts who hold a master's or Ph.D. degree should find good opportunities through the year 2005. The number of openings generated each year as a result of employment growth and the need to replace those leaving the occupation is expected to exceed the number of persons graduating with master's and Ph.D. degrees from management science or operations research programs.

Graduates with only a bachelor's degree in operations research or management science should find opportunities as research assistants or analyst assistants in a variety of related fields that allow them to use their quantitative abilities. Only the most highly qualified are likely to find employment as operations research or management science analysts.

Employment of operations research analysts is expected to grow much faster than the average for all occupations due to the increasing importance of quantitative analysis in decision-making. Much of the job growth is expected to occur in the transportation, manufacturing, finance, and service sectors, areas where the use of quantitative analysis can achieve dramatic improvements in operating efficiency and profitability. More airlines, for example, are using operations research to determine the best flight and maintenance schedules, select the best routes to service, analyze customer characteristics, and control fuel consumption, among other things. Motel chains are beginning to use operations research to improve their efficiency by analyzing automobile traffic patterns and customer attitudes to determine location, size, and style of proposed new motels. Like other management support functions, operations research grows by its own success. When one firm in an industry increases productivity by adopting a new procedure, its competitors usually follow. This competitive pressure will contribute to demand for operations research analysts.

Demand also should be strong in the manufacturing sector as firms expand existing operations research staffs in the face of growing domestic and foreign competition. More manufacturers are using mathematical models to study the operations of the organization. For example, analysts will be needed to determine the best way to control product inventory, distribute finished products, and decide where sales offices should be based. In addition, increasing factory automation will require more operations research analysts to alter existing models or develop new ones for production layout, robotics installation, work schedules, and inventory control.

PROFESSIONAL ASSOCIATIONS

Institute for Operations Research and the Management Sciences
290 Westminster Street
Providence, RI 02903

Military Operations Research Society
101 South Whiting Street, Suite 202
Alexandria, VA 22304

Operations Research Society of America
1314 Guilford Avenue
Baltimore, MD 21202

CHAPTER THIRTEEN

PATH 4: COMPUTER OPERATORS AND PROGRAMMERS

"If it keeps up, man will atrophy all his limbs but the push-button finger."

—Frank Lloyd Wright

HELP WANTED

Computer Operator
2nd Shift

Our manufacturing company has an opening for a 2nd shift computer operator. We are a leading designer and manufacturer of electrical equipment, components, and controls that provide for the economical, safe, and reliable delivery of high-quality electrical power.

High school diploma and 2+ years' experience as a computer operator is required. We also seek a background in IBM Mainframe—VSE/SP—and knowledge of VTAM commands. Familiarity with XBMS software is a plus, but not required.

Send resume in confidence.

DEFINITION OF THE CAREER PATH

Computer Operators

HELP WANTED

Computer Operators
1st and 3rd Shifts
Locally based international marketing firm seeks computer operators with entry-level programming skills. Must have working knowledge of FoxBASE/DBase and/or FoxPro. Knowledge of UNIX a plus. Duties will include database file processing in a DOS and UNIX environment. Send resumes.

Computer and peripheral equipment operators oversee the operation of computer hardware systems, ensuring that these machines are used as efficiently as possible. This means that operators must be proactive—anticipate problems before they occur and take preventive action as well as solve problems that do occur.

Duties of computer and peripheral equipment operators vary with the policies of the employer, the size of the installation, and the kind of equipment used. Working from operating instructions prepared by programmers, users, or operations managers, computer operators set controls on the computer and on peripheral devices required to run a particular job. Computer operators, or, in some large installations, peripheral equipment operators, load the equipment with tapes, disks, and paper as needed. While the computer is running (which may be 24 hours a day for large computers), computer operators monitor the computer console and respond to operating and computer messages. Messages indicate the individual specifications of each job being run. If an error message occurs, operators must locate and solve the problem or terminate the program.

Traditionally, peripheral equipment operators have to prepare printouts and other output for distribution to computer users. Operators also maintain log books listing each job that is run and events such as machine malfunctions that occurred during their shift. In addition, computer operators may supervise and train peripheral equipment operators and computer operator trainees. They also may help programmers and systems analysts test and debug new programs.

As the trend toward networking computers accelerates, a growing number of these workers are operating personal computers (PCs) and minicomputers. More and more, establishments are recognizing the need to connect all their computers in order to enhance productivity. In many offices, factories, and other work settings, PCs and minicomputers serve as the center of such networks, often referred to as local area networks or multiuser systems. While some of these computers are operated by users in the area, many require the services of full-time operators. The tasks performed are very similar to those performed on the larger computers.

As organizations continue to use computers in more areas of operation, they are also fulfilling opportunities to increase the productivity of computer operations. Automation, which traditionally has been the application of computer technology to other functional areas of an organization, is now reaching the computer room. Sophisticated software coupled with robotics now exist, enabling the computer to perform many routine tasks formerly done by computer and peripheral equipment operators. Scheduling, loading and downloading programs, mounting tapes, rerouting messages, and running periodic reports can be done without the intervention of an operator. These improvements will change what computer operators do in the future. However, in the computer centers that lack this level of automation, some computer operators still may be responsible for tasks traditionally done by peripheral equipment operators. As technology advances, many computer operators will essentially monitor an automated system. As the role of operators changes due to new technology, their responsibilities may shift to system security, troubleshooting, desk help, network problems, and maintaining large databases.

Computer/console operators operate and monitor computer runs. They follow the programmers' instructions for processing the data that goes into the computer. They make sure that the computer has been loaded with the correct magnetic tape or disks and watch closely for error lights which indicate that the computer is not operating properly.

Computer Programmers

> **HELP WANTED**
>
> **Programmers**
> Our successful consulting firm is expanding into the computer consulting market. Highest hourly rates paid for experienced developers. Benefits include major medical, life, dental, and vision. Join a growing company. If you have been on your job for three to five years and believe you are underpaid, you need to contact us. Send resume.

Computer programmers write and maintain the detailed instructions, called *programs* or *software,* that list, in a logical order, the steps that computers must execute to perform their functions. In many large organizations, programmers follow descriptions prepared by systems analysts who have carefully studied the task that the computer system is going to perform. These descriptions list the input required, the steps the computer must follow to process data, and the desired arrangement of the output. Some organizations, particularly smaller ones, do not employ systems analysts. Instead, workers called programmer-analysts are responsible for both systems analysis and programming.

Regardless of setting, programmers write specific programs by breaking down each step into a logical series of instructions the computer can follow. They then code these instructions in a conventional programming language, such as C or FORTRAN, or one of the more advanced Artificial Intelligence or object oriented languages, such as LISP, Prolog, C++, or Ada.

The transition from a mainframe environment to primarily a PC-based environment has blurred the once rigid distinction between the programmer and the user. Increasingly, adept users are taking over many of the tasks previously performed by programmers. For example, the growing use of packaged software, such as spreadsheet and database management software packages, allows users to write simple programs to access data and perform calculations.

Programmers in software development companies may work directly with experts from various fields to create software, either programs designed for specific clients or packaged software for general use, ranging from games and educational software to programs for desktop publishing, financial planning, and spreadsheets. Much of the programming being done today is in the area of packaged software development, one of the most rapidly growing segments of the computer industry.

Despite the prevalence of packaged software, many programmers are involved in updating, debugging, and modifying code for existing programs. When making changes to a section of code, called a *routine,* programmers need to make other users aware of the task that the routine is to perform. They do this by inserting comments in the coded instructions so others can understand the program. Programmers using computer-aided software engineering (CASE) tools can concentrate on writing the unique parts of the program because the tools automate various pieces of the program being built. This also yields more reliable and consistent programs and increases programmers' productivity by eliminating some of the routine steps.

When a program is ready to be tested, programmers give it a *test run* to ensure that the instructions are correct and will produce the desired information. They prepare sample data that test every part of the program and, after trial runs, review the results to see if any errors were made. If errors do occur, the programmer must make the appropriate modifications and recheck the program until it produces the desired results. This is what is known as *debugging* the program.

Finally, programmers working in a mainframe environment prepare instructions for the computer operator who will run the program.

Programs vary depending upon the type of information to be accessed or generated. For example, the instructions involved in updating financial records are different from those required to duplicate conditions onboard an aircraft for pilots training in a flight simulator. Although simple programs can be written in a few hours, programs that use complex mathematical formulas or many data files may require more than a year of work. In most cases, several programmers may work together as a team under a senior programmer's supervision.

Programmers often are grouped into two broad types: applications programmers and systems programmers. Applications programmers usually are oriented toward business, engineering, or science. They write software designed to handle specific jobs, such as a program used in an inventory control system or one to guide a missile after it has been fired. They also may work alone to revise existing packaged software. Systems programmers, on the other hand, maintain the software that controls the operation of an entire computer system. These workers make changes in the sets of instructions that determine how the central processing unit of the system handles the various jobs it has been given and communicates with peripheral equipment, such as terminals, printers, and disk drives. Because of their knowledge of the entire computer system, systems programmers often help applications programmers determine the source of problems that may occur with their programs.

POSSIBLE JOB TITLES

Computer operator

Computer programmer

HELP WANTED

Programmers
Stuck in the Slow Lane?
Join one of the fastest growing CASE and client/server consulting firms in the United States. We are an established international consulting firm that is growing at 60 percent annually, so you can advance as fast as your ambition allows. Our nine-week

continued

continued

training program will get you moving on the fast track. Candidates should have a solid technical skill set, including several programming languages, a computer-related Bachelor of Science Degree, and one to two years experience. Knowledge of CASE or client/server tools not required—but a plus. 100 percent travel offers an outstanding opportunity to see the world. All travel expenses paid, excellent compensation package, bonus for consultants. Fax resumes.

POSSIBLE EMPLOYERS

Computer operators and peripheral equipment operators hold about 259,000 and 30,000 jobs, respectively. Although jobs for computer and peripheral equipment operators are found in almost every industry, most are in data processing service firms; wholesale trade establishments; manufacturing companies; financial institutions; and government agencies. These organizations have data processing needs that require large computer installations. A growing number are employed by firms in the computer and data processing services industry, as more companies contract out the operation of their data processing centers.

More than one out of ten computer and peripheral equipment operators work part time.

Computer programmers hold about 537,000 jobs. They are employed in most industries, with the largest concentrations in computer and office equipment manufacturing, data processing service organizations, firms that write and sell software, companies that provide engineering and management services, financial institutions, insurance carriers, and government agencies. Applications programmers work for all types of firms, whereas systems programmers usually work for organizations with large computer centers or for firms that manufacture computers or develop software.

A growing number of programmers are employed on a temporary or contract basis. Rather than hiring programmers as permanent employees and then laying them off after a job is completed, employers increasingly are contracting with temporary help agencies, consulting firms, or directly with programmers themselves. A marketing firm, for example, may only require the services of several programmers to write and debug the software necessary to get a new database management system running. Such jobs may last for several months to a year or longer.

> **HELP WANTED**
>
> **Programmer**
> We are a national provider of practice management software to the medical community.
>
> We are currently seeking an experienced Database Programmer to work in the UNIX environment writing custom programs, conversions, and interfaces to our software. Qualified applicants will possess a BSCS and three to five years database programming experience. Medical Manager/Data Merge experience a definite plus.
>
> We offer excellent working conditions and competitive compensation. Please fax resume.

RELATED OCCUPATIONS

Other occupations involving interaction with computers include computer scientists, systems analysts, and computer service technicians. Other jobs in which workers operate electronic office equipment include data entry keyers, secretaries, typists and word processors, and typesetters and compositors.

Programmers must pay great attention to detail as they write and debug programs. Other professional workers who must be detail oriented include statisticians, engineers, financial analysts, accountants, auditors, actuaries, and operations research analysts.

> **HELP WANTED**
>
> **Computer Operator—Full Time**
> Bank is seeking an experienced computer operator. Requirements are: a strong knowledge of the IBM, AS 400 Computer System, ability to meet deadlines. Excellent attendance and punctuality and experience operating 3892 Reader Sorters. If you meet these qualifications, please send resume including salary history.

WORKING CONDITIONS

Computer operators usually work approximately 35 to 40 hours per week in well-lighted, well-ventilated, comfortable rooms. Because many organizations use their computers 24 hours a day, seven days a week, computer and peripheral equipment operators may be required to work evening or night shifts and weekends. Shift assignments generally are made on the basis of seniority. Automated operations will lessen the need for shift work because many companies let the computer take over all operations during less desirable working hours.

Because computer operators spend a lot of time in front of a computer monitor, as well as performing repetitive tasks such as loading and unloading printers, they may be susceptible to eyestrain, back discomfort, and hand and wrist problems.

Computer programmers usually work in offices that are clean and comfortable. Working hours usually number 35 to 40 hours per week; but not necessarily nine o'clock to five o'clock. Regular schedules may include evening or weekend hours. In addition, programmers may work longer hours or on weekends in order to meet deadlines or fix critical problems that occur during off hours.

Because programmers also spend long periods of time in front of a computer monitor typing at a keyboard, they too are susceptible to eyestrain, back discomfort, and hand and wrist problems.

HELP WANTED

Computer Programmer
International company seeking professional with knowledge of Visual Basic, FoxPro, and Novell network. The chosen candidate will streamline computer department operations. Good salary and benefits for the right person. Call to arrange interview.

TRAINING AND QUALIFICATIONS

Previous work experience is the key to landing an operator job in many large establishments. Employers look for specific, hands-on experience in the type of equipment and related operating systems that they use. Additionally, computer-related formal training, perhaps through a junior college or technical school, is recommended. As computer technology changes and data processing centers become more automated, more employers will require candidates for the remaining operator jobs to have formal training as well as experience.

Workers usually receive on-the-job training in order to become acquainted with their employer's equipment and routines. The length of training varies with the job and the experience of the worker. Training is also offered by the armed forces and by some computer manufacturers.

Because computer technology changes so rapidly, operators must be adaptable and willing to learn. Greater analytical and technical expertise are also needed to deal with the unique or higher-level problems that the computer is not programmed to handle, particularly by operators who work in automated data centers.

Computer and peripheral equipment operators must be able to communicate well in order to work effectively with programmers or users, as well as with other operators. Computer operators also must be able to work independently because they may have little or no supervision.

Peripheral equipment operators may advance to computer operator jobs. A few computer operators may advance to supervisory jobs. Through on-the-job experience and additional formal education, some computer and peripheral equipment operators may advance to jobs as programmers or analysts, although the move into these jobs is becoming more difficult as employers increasingly require candidates for more skilled computer professional jobs to possess at least a bachelor's degree. Others may become specialists in areas such as network operations or support.

There are no universal training requirements for programmers because employers' needs are so varied. Computer applications have become so widespread that computer programming is taught at most public and private vocational schools, community and junior colleges, and universities. However, the level of education and quality of training that employers seek have been rising due to the growth in the number of qualified applicants and the increasing complexity of some programming tasks. Although some programmers obtain two-year degrees or certificates, bachelor's degrees are now commonly required. Candidates usually have earned a bachelor of arts or bachelor of science degree, often in computer science or information systems. Graduate degrees are required for some jobs. Employers who use computers for business applications prefer to hire people who have had college courses in management information systems (MIS) and business, and who possess strong programming skills. Knowledge of FORTRAN, COBOL, C, Fourth Generation Languages (4GL), CASE tools, systems programming, C++, Smalltalk, and other object-oriented programming languages is highly desirable. General business skills and experience related to the operations of the firm are preferred by employers as well.

Most systems programmers hold a four-year degree in computer science. Extensive knowledge of a variety of operating systems is essential. This includes being able to configure the operating system to work with different types of hardware, and adapting the operating system to best meet the needs of the particular organization. They also must be able to work with database systems such as DB2, Oracle, or Sybase, for example.

The Institute for Certification of Computing Professionals confers the designation Certified Computing Professional (CCP) to those who have at least four years of experience or two years of experience and a college degree. To qualify, individuals must pass a core examination plus exams in two specialty areas, or an exam in one specialty area and two computing languages. Those with little or no experience may be tested for certification as an Associate Computer Professional (ACP). Certification is not mandatory, but it may give a job seeker a competitive advantage.

When hiring programmers, employers look for people with the necessary programming skills who can think logically and pay close attention to detail. The job calls for patience, persistence, and the ability to do exacting analytical work, especially under pressure. Ingenuity and imagination are also particularly important when programmers design solutions and test their work for potential failures. Increasingly, interpersonal skills are important as programmers are expected to work in teams and interact directly with users. The ability to work with abstract concepts and do technical analysis is especially important for systems programmers because they work with the software that controls the computer's operation.

Beginning programmers may spend their first weeks on the job attending training classes since each business has its own development methodology, processes, and tools. After this initial instruction, they may work alone on simple assignments, or on a team with more experienced programmers. Either way, they generally must spend at least several months working under close supervision. Because of rapidly changing technology, programmers must continuously update their training by taking courses sponsored by their employer or software vendors.

For skilled workers, the prospects for advancement are good. In large organizations, they may be promoted to lead programmer and be given supervisory responsibilities. Some applications programmers may move into systems programming after they gain experience and take courses in systems software. With general business experience, both applications programmers and systems programmers may become systems analysts or be promoted to a managerial position. Other programmers, with specialized knowledge and experience with a language or operating system, may work in research and development areas such as multimedia or Internet technology. As employers increasingly contract out programming jobs, more opportunities should arise for experienced programmers with expertise in a specific area to work as consultants.

HELP WANTED

Programmer

We are a leader in the education industry and have been for more than 120 years. We are seeking an experienced programmer for our local facility. You'll be responsible for developing, testing,

continued

continued

maintaining, and troubleshooting a variety of platforms, including ES9000 and RS6000. Ideal candidate will have the ability to work well on a team and independently. Position requires a Bachelor's Degree in Computer Science or a related field, experience, one to two years of COBOL programming experience, and good communication skills. Programming in Natural and design skills desirable. Will consider a new graduate. Our working environment is business-casual, and we provide many excellent benefits including 401(k), profit sharing, and medical/dental insurance. Please forward resume.

EARNINGS

Recent studies indicate that full-time computer operators have a median income of $21,300 a year. The middle 50 percent earn between $16,200 and $29,900. The lowest 10 percent earn less than $12,800 and the top 10 percent earn more than $39,500.

According to Robert Half International Inc., the average starting salaries for computer operators range from $20,000 to $31,500. Salaries generally are higher in large organizations than in small ones.

In the federal government, computer operators with a high school diploma start at about $14,900 a year. Those with a year of college start at $16,700. Applicants with operations experience start at higher salaries. The average annual salary for all computer operators employed by the federal government in nonsupervisory, supervisory, and managerial positions is about $28,800.

Median earnings of programmers who work full time is about $38,400 a year. The middle 50 percent earn between about $30,000 and $49,200 a year. The lowest 10 percent earn less than $22,000, and the highest 10 percent, more than $60,600.

According to Robert Half International Inc., starting salaries in large establishments for 1994 range from $29,500 to $36,500 for programmers; $36,000 to $47,000 for programmer analysts; and $44,000 to $54,000 for systems programmers. Starting salaries in small establishments range from $25,000 to $34,000 for programmers and from $30,000 to $40,000 for programmer analysts.

Salaries and benefits for computer programmers are generally higher than those earned by nonsupervisory workers in other fields. Most companies offer paid vacations and holidays along with sick leave and medical insurance. Other benefits offered might be pension plans, profit sharing, and tuition reimbursement.

Programmers working in the West and Northeast earn somewhat more than those working in the South and Midwest. On average, systems programmers earn more than applications programmers.

In the federal government, the entrance salary for programmers with a college degree or qualifying experience is about $18,700 a year. Those with a superior academic record may earn $23,200.

CAREER OUTLOOK

Employment of computer and peripheral equipment operators is expected to decline sharply through the year 2005. Many experienced operators are expected to compete for the small number of openings that will arise each year to replace workers who transfer to other occupations or leave the labor force.

Advances in technology have reduced both the size and the cost of computer equipment while increasing the capacity for data storage and processing. These improvements in technology have fueled an expansion in the use of computers in such areas as factory and office automation, telecommunications, medicine, and education.

The expanding use of software that automates computer operations gives companies the option of making systems user-friendly, greatly reducing the need for operators. Even if firms continue to employ operators in some capacity—which, for many, is extremely likely in the near future—these new technologies will require operators to monitor a greater number of operations at the same time and be capable of solving a broader range of problems that may arise. The result is that fewer and fewer operators will be needed to perform more highly skilled work.

Computer operators or peripheral equipment operators who are displaced by automation may be reassigned to support staffs that maintain personal computer networks or assist other members of the organization. Operators who keep up with changing technology, by updating their skills and enhancing their training, should have the best prospects of moving into other areas such as network administration. Others may be retrained to perform different job duties, such as supervising an entire operations center, maintaining automation packages, or analyzing computer operations to recommend ways to increase productivity. In the future, operators who wish to continue in the computer field will need to know more about programming, automation software, graphics interfaces, and open systems in order to take advantage of changing opportunities.

Employment of programmers is expected to grow about as fast as the average for all occupations through the year 2005. Employment is not expected to grow as rapidly as in the past as improved software and programming techniques continue to simplify programming tasks. In addition, greater use of packaged software—such as word processing and spreadsheet packages—should continue to moderate the growth in demand for applications programmers. As the level of technological innovation and sophistication increases, users will be able to design, write, and implement more of their own programs to meet their changing needs.

Although the proportion of programmers leaving the occupation each year is smaller than that of most occupations, most of the job openings for programmers will result from replacement needs. The majority of programmers who leave transfer to other occupations, such as manager or systems analyst. Jobs for both systems and applications programmers, however, should remain particularly plentiful in data processing service firms, software houses, and computer consulting businesses. These types of establishments remain part of one of the fastest-growing industries—computer and data processing services. As companies look to control costs, those in need of programming services should look to this industry to meet these needs.

As computer usage expands, however, the demand for skilled programmers will increase as organizations seek new applications for computers and improvements to the software already in use. Employers are increasingly interested in programmers who can combine areas of technical expertise or who are adaptable and able to learn and incorporate new skills. One area of progress will be data communications. Networking computers so they can communicate with each other is necessary to achieve the greater efficiency that organizations require to remain competitive. Object-oriented languages will increasingly be used in the years ahead, further enhancing the productivity of programmers. Programmers will be creating and maintaining expert systems and embedding these technologies in more and more products.

STRATEGY FOR FINDING THE JOBS

The number and quality of applicants for programmer jobs have increased, so employers have become more selective. Graduates of two-year programs in data processing, and people with less than a two-year degree or its equivalent in work experience, are facing especially strong competition for programming jobs. Competition for entry-level positions even affects applicants with a bachelor's degree. Many observers expect opportunities for people without college degrees to diminish in coming years as programming tasks become more complex and more sophisticated skills and experience are demanded by employers. Prospects should be good for college graduates with knowledge of a variety of programming languages, particularly C++ and other object-oriented languages, as well as newer languages that apply to computer networking, database management, and artificial intelligence. In order to remain competitive, college graduates should keep up-to-date with the latest skills and technologies.

Many employers prefer to hire applicants with previous experience in the field. Firms also desire programmers who develop a technical specialization in areas such as client/server programming, multimedia technology, graphic user interface, or fourth- and fifth-generation programming tools. Therefore, people who want to become programmers can enhance their chances by combining work experience with the appropriate formal training. Students should try to gain experience by participating in a college work-study program, or undertaking an internship. Students also can greatly improve their employment prospects by taking courses such as accounting, management, engineering, or science-allied fields in which applications programmers are in demand. With the expansion of client/server environments, employers will continue to look for programmers with strong technical skills, as well as good interpersonal and business skills.

PROFESSIONAL ASSOCIATIONS

Association for Computing Machinery
1515 Broadway
New York, NY 10036

Association of Computer Professionals
1515 Broadway
New York, NY 10036

Institute for the Certification of Computing Professionals
2200 East Devon Avenue, Suite 268
Des Plaines, IL 60018

National Systems Programmers Association
4811 South 76th Street
Milwaukee, WI 53220

MEET KATHY HARGREAVES

Kathy Hargreaves earned a bachelor of arts degree from UCLA, an M.F.A. from UCLA (both in painting/sculpture/graphic arts), and an M.A. in computer science from the University of Massachusetts in Boston. She has worked as a self-employed software consultant since 1989.

"I was turned to computers by a very enthusiastic boss from my first real job after college," she says. "We were both art graduates, so the technical world was very esoteric. Of course, I was completely terrified of the whole technical thing. Later, I began working as a typesetter in a big firm in San Francisco. The individual who was setting up and programming the computer system waltzed in at 11:00 A.M., while we had to punch time clocks! The work was already close to what I later found out was writing macros, and I'd already been taking programming courses so I found out about a reentry program for women and minorities at a local university and decided to go for it.

"Now, I work at home mostly," she says. "If I'm working hourly, it's harder to not go overboard with the hours than you might think. I try to restrict programming to the morning. Basically, I get up, eat breakfast, and go upstairs to the computer until it's time to exercise.

"Work ranges from simple typing to writing macros in typesetting language. I try to stay relaxed about it. Basically, I avoid strict deadline jobs so I can control the hours that I work. In total, I work about 20 to 30 hours per week.

"I enjoy working out of my house and make good use of the phone and e-mail to keep in touch with my clients," she says.

"I really like not having to deal with a boss face-to-face or go into an office (often without windows that open) for set times of the day. I enjoy the fact that I don't have to deal with the hassle of commuting to work. On the other hand, I least like having to find work, clients who don't answer e-mail or make it clear what they want and for how much. Or those who don't even know what they want.

"I'd advise others who are considering this type of work to avoid this occupation unless you really love doing it."

CHAPTER FOURTEEN

PATH 5: COMPUTER SALES AND SERVICE

"A computer will do what you tell it to do, but that may be different from what you had in mind."

—Joseph Weizenbaum, quoted in *Time*

HELP WANTED

Computer Network Sales Consultant

Are you someone who enjoys assessing business needs and providing solutions?

We require:

- Strong technical knowledge
- College degree
- 1–3 years experience

Send resume immediately!

DEFINITION OF THE CAREER PATH

Computer Sales

Success in a sales career (in any field) requires knowledge of the product or service being offered, in addition to expertise in the art of selling. Thus, individuals interested in a career in computer sales need to learn everything possible about computers and how they operate, in addition to gaining sufficient knowledge and understanding of the psychology of sales.

All salespeople must be able to convince prospective customers of the value of their products and services. This involves demonstrating the equipment and pointing out its design and engineering superiority and the various advantages it provides the consumer over competitive products in the marketplace. In order to accomplish this, sales professionals need to possess a thorough familiarity with electronics and a firm grasp of the particulars involved in the line of computers and the kinds of software on the market. These are the products that will enable the user to accomplish such tasks as billing, word processing, accounting, and so on.

There is a fundamental difference between computer salespeople who work in a store and those who are involved in outside sales. In the first case, customers already have some interest and have been drawn into a store, either because of word of mouth; special promotions; or ads the company may have placed in newspapers, on radio, or on TV.

This is not to intimate, however, that retail sales clerks must not actively make use of selling expertise, because they certainly do. Interested parties still must be converted to customers. In some cases, salespeople may succeed in upgrading a prospective customer from an inexpensive, beginning-level personal computer to one that can do more sophisticated applications in a fraction of the time. They can also be instrumental in selling customers peripheral and add-on equipment that they will need for their computers—more sophisticated or color video display terminals, for instance, modems for telephone transmission of computer messages, surge protectors to guard against power surges, cables, and of course software, depending upon what the customer wants to do with the computer.

Outside salespeople, on the other hand, must usually work primarily on their own, developing their own lists of prospects, working from leads supplied by the company via mail, fax, e-mail, or phone. In addition to this, these sales professionals must be able to develop lists of prospective clients to call on through the use of phone books and business directories, chamber of commerce directories, and other reference materials. Further, they may seek leads from their business associates, personal connections, satisfied customers, trade publications, and anywhere else they can think of.

HELP WANTED

Software Sales
Dynamic self-starter to sell automated data collection solutions to installed base of manufacturing software for fast-growing supplier of systems and services. Minimum 5 years experience and 3 years manufacturing solution sales experience required. Data collection experience a plus. Please mail or fax resume.

Whatever the source of the lead, the sales professional may have to visit the client's office to demonstrate the computer system to all involved, including the person who may be using the computer, the department supervisor, the person who must approve the purchase, and any other interested persons. Often the salesperson may have to make one or more return trips to make a sale.

Computer Service

HELP WANTED

Computer Technician

AA degree in computer science or related field or currently pursuing a degree

Contractual employment—$9.25 to $11.50 per hour/benefits

Experience installing computer and computer peripherals

Need valid driver's license and car

Start immediately

Interested individuals should complete an application or submit a letter of inquiry with supporting data.

Computer repairers install equipment, do preventive maintenance, and correct problems. They work on computers (mainframes, minis, and micros), peripheral equipment, and word processing systems. Some repairers service both computers and office equipment. They may make cable and wiring connections when installing equipment, and work closely with electricians, who install the wiring.

Even with preventive maintenance, computers and other machines do break down. Repairers run diagnostic programs to locate malfunctions. Although some of the most modern and sophisticated computers have a self-diagnosing capacity that identifies problems, computer repairers must know enough about systems software to determine if the malfunction is in the hardware or in the software.

HELP WANTED

Computer Service Rep

Progressive computer rental services company is seeking a customer service oriented driver to deliver and install computer equipment. Knowledge of DOS, Windows, and Apple operating systems required along with a degree in computer science or a related field. A clean driving record and valid driver's license also required. Send resume.

POSSIBLE JOB TITLES

Account executive

Computer account representative

Computer salesperson

Computer service person

Computer technician

Retail store manager

POSSIBLE EMPLOYERS

Jobs in computer sales fall into two categories: 1. employment by vendors or manufacturers and 2. jobs in retail stores. Vendors sell directly to the industry. They try to meet the needs of computer users such as banks, insurance companies, colleges and universities and school systems, accounting and business agencies, hospitals and health-care facilities, government agencies, and others in all sectors of the economy. Sales personnel may work out of the vendor's headquarters, or be assigned to district sales offices throughout the country.

With the proliferation of PCs in the home and industry, computers are now sold in thousands of retail establishments located all over the country. These include computer stores, office equipment stores, department stores, furniture and appliance dealers, as well as independent sales organizations that sell directly to industry, including value-added resellers (VARs), system integrators, and others who serve as consultants and agents in matching computer systems to the needs of commercial and industrial firms.

Some of the large computer stores also have outside sales forces who call upon schools, industrial firms, and government agencies, as well as catalog or mail-order divisions that take orders over the phone from customers who have received the company's catalog.

Computer and office machine repairers hold about 134,000 jobs. Approximately 75,000 work mainly on computer equipment, and the other 59,000 repair mainly office machines. Three of every five are employed by wholesalers of computers and other office equipment, including the wholesaling divisions of equipment manufacturers, and by firms that provide maintenance services for a fee. Others work for retail establishments and some with organizations that service their own equipment.

Repairers work throughout the country, even in relatively small communities. Most repairers, however, work in large cities, where computer and office equipment is concentrated.

RELATED OCCUPATIONS

Individuals involved in selling computers can transfer their expertise to sell almost any product or service, particularly those in the area of technology. Sales professionals perform similar tasks to travel agents, real estate agents, insurance agents, financial representatives, and advertising account executives. Those involved in service can also transfer their skills to servicing any other type of product, particularly one involving electronics or technology.

HELP WANTED

Computer Marketing Rep

Seeking an enthusiastic professional field sales rep with strong technology background. Retail channel experience a plus. Degree in marketing, sales, or computer science desired. Must have exceptional presentation skills, be capable of managing a territory, and be able to clearly communicate technical information. Responsibilities will include sales, training, and account management for cutting edge PC products from one of the world's largest technology companies.

WORKING CONDITIONS

Those involved in computer sales, particularly retail sales, may work peak hours including evenings and weekends. Usually a 40-hour week is assigned except during special sales or promotions when additional hours may be expected.

Computer service personnel usually work 40 hours per week in a variety of offices, some of which they may have to travel to. In emergency situations, overtime may be necessary. Shift work is not uncommon. Some are on call 24 hours.

HELP WANTED

Computer Service Technician
Growing computer company looking for a field service technician. Qualifications are: reliable transportation, communication
skills, eagerness to learn new technologies, and knowledgeable
about PCs, printers, software, and LANs. Knowledge of Novell a
definite plus. We offer a competitive salary and benefits for full-
time employees. Fax resume.

TRAINING AND QUALIFICATIONS

While you do not necessarily have to have a college degree to get a job in retail sales, it will be a definite plus, not only in securing the job and performing it well, but in advancing to higher and better-paying jobs. The core curriculum for college or university centers upon courses in computer science. Besides this concentration, you should take required and elective courses in math (differential and integral calculus, analytical geometry, and applied modern algebra), natural sciences (physics is especially important), the humanities (literature, art, and history), and the social sciences. Also important are business courses such as marketing and sales. A knowledge of speech communication or public speaking can help you in making presentations before small and large groups. More than 75 percent of those currently involved in computer sales, both in the retail and corporate levels, are college graduates.

Look into the availability of PC users' clubs. By joining and participating in such groups, you can become more familiar with computer terminology and procedures, which will help you when you begin to look for employment in the industry.

Success in sales is based largely on how well you understand people—what motivates them, and why they buy. Thus, exposure to the public can be invaluable in learning how to deal successfully with people. You must be ambitious, aggressive, independent, organized, detail-minded, an able listener, and a good communicator. If you are truly computer savvy, you will be able to ascertain the customer's needs and provide a viable solution.

Because of the need to keep abreast of all of the most recent developments in the field, the sales representative may periodically be expected to attend seminars on the use of the product and on software systems or applications as they are developed. Such seminars may be offered by the employers or vendor, or by the manufacturers in the case of business-to-business sales. Such sales training programs can range from a few days in the case of a retail store, to several months of intensive training in the case of a large vendor. These sessions are supplemented by small sales meetings of a day or two, stressing new products and applications in the case of the retail store, and new features of the product or computer system in the case of the vendor.

In addition to this, retail sales employees, and to a certain extent vendor sales reps, are expected to know how to handle the paperwork involved in making out sales records, receiving cash, handling charge slips, coupons, and so on. Sales personnel may also be expected to handle returns and exchanges, help stock shelves, make price tags, put up displays, and help take inventory. But the bottom line is doing whatever is necessary to satisfy the customer or client.

To perform service on computers, employers will seek candidates with a minimum of a high school education plus training in electronics and course work in mathematics, science, and electronics. Many companies prefer several years of electronics at a technical school or college and/or practical experience.

Personal attributes include good vision (with no color blindness) and the ability to work long hours and to deal with stress. Desirable qualities also include the ability to deal well with customers, to explain details, and to work with little supervision. Candidates should be mechanically skillful, interested in electronics, and able to complete precise work with manual dexterity.

EARNINGS

Earnings vary widely for sales personnel depending on performance. Experienced sales reps can earn over $100,000 a year, more than their management superiors. The median income of sales reps (often based on a combination of straight salary and commission) is about $25,000 to $35,000 per year. Outside salespeople earn median salaries of $45,000 to $60,000 per year. Median salaries for inside sales personnel is about $30,000. Benefits are also important—some companies offer paid vacations, health insurance, retirement plans, bonuses, extra vacation time, trips, and prizes for bettering company quotas.

The *Occupational Outlook Handbook* created by the United States Department of Labor reports that average salaries for service technicians are about $575 per week. The middle 50 percent falls between $434 and $765; the bottom 10 percent less than $317, and the top 10 percent more than $947.

CAREER OUTLOOK

With the popularity of computers continuing to increase at a steady rate, opportunities are excellent for individuals interested in embarking on careers in computer sales. For those with at least a bachelor's degree, experience in sales (of any kind), and knowledge of computers and the computer world, the chances of employment are especially good. Larger cities provide increased opportunities.

Employment of computer and office machine repairers is expected to grow faster than the average for all occupations through the year 2005. Demand for computer repairers will increase as the amount of computer equipment increases. Organizations throughout the economy should continue to automate in search of greater productivity and improved service. The development of new computer applications and lower computer prices will also spur demand. More repairers will be needed to install, maintain, and repair these machines.

Computer and office machine repairers work throughout the country, even in relatively small communities.

PROFESSIONAL ASSOCIATIONS

Association for Computing Machinery
11 West 42nd Street
New York, NY 10036

Communications Workers of America
501 3rd Street, NW
Washington, DC 20001

Computer and Communications Industry Association
666 11th Street, NW
Washington, DC 20001

Computer Dealers and Lessors Association
1212 Potomac Street, NW
Washington, DC 20007

Electronics Technicians Association
604 North Jackson
Greencastle, IN 46135

United States Telephone Association
1401 H Street, NW, Suite 600
Washington, DC 20005-2136

MEET MARTY GORELICK

Marty Gorelick has a bachelor of arts degree from Long Island University in New York, and eight years experience in computer hardware sales. He has also attended seminars from all of the major computer manufacturers: Compaq, IBM, Hewlett Packard, Sony, Apple, and NEC. He is account manager for County Government Sales at GE Capital IT Solutions in Miami, Florida, where he services Metro-Dade, Broward County, and Pasco County plus all cities, towns, and villages within these municipalities.

"The computer industry is constantly changing," he says. "It is the fastest-growing industry in the world. Every person on our planet is connected in one way or another. Computers have made communications possible at lightning speed.

"Scientists, doctors, engineers, lawyers, manufacturers, teachers, those in the arts, and every other element of our society operates at higher levels of proficiency than ever before because of computers. For example, a doctor in Seattle can supervise a surgical procedure in an operating room located in Atlanta through the aid of a computer hookup. Ten short years ago, this was impossible. Using a process called computer-aided design (CAD), engineers can design structures that will withstand stress far beyond their intended safety limits. Police can track known law offenders well outside of their jurisdiction and notify other law enforcement officers of potential problems. This, by far, is only the tip of the iceberg. Computer applications are endless.

"A typical day for me begins when I arrive at my office about 6:30 A.M. After running the branch's allocation reports for all the salespeople in our office, I check my voice mail for any emergency issues that must be addressed quickly. An example might be a critical shipment that hasn't arrived on time or a file server that has developed a problem and is inoperable. These situations demand my immediate attention. If both these situations exist, I'll contact our Atlanta facility to run a tracer and our service department to check out the server on their first call of the day.

"I read my e-mail messages next. It's not unusual to have between five and fifteen messages ranging from company updates to manufacturer price changes, to additions and deletions from any number of vendors. Since I give my e-mail address to my customers, I might see a request for a quotation on a product or clarification of a service agreement or a question about the configuration of a mini-tower

continued

continued

computer with 32 MB memory, 2.5 GB hard drive, and an 8X CD-ROM. Some messages require a response A.S.A.P., others can be addressed during the course of my regular business day.

"Next stop is my in-mail box, which usually contains a collection of faxes that have arrived since I left the office at the end of business yesterday. These faxes could contain purchase orders, manufacturer promotional notices, seminar information, or news of a prospective customer looking for a great reseller like ours! All this, and the clock has not yet struck 8:00 A.M.

"Now, the doors swing open and my fellow employees arrive. The phones go off night ring and our customers start calling in. We field calls concerning products, service, availability, additions, deletions, and changes in orders.

"During the course of the day, the staff may all assemble for a quick meeting to discuss a change in plans concerning a new company procedure. (Our regularly scheduled sales meeting takes place at 8:30 A.M. sharp each Wednesday. This is when we discuss our progress as a group and host a manufacturer who is introducing a new product or products.)

"We constantly update our price list to remain the most competitive reseller in the marketplace. I do a special electronic price list for the county every sixty days. This process usually takes me anywhere from three to four working days. I also provide a manuscript of 5,000-plus items from a third-party vendor. On any given day, I may accompany a manufacturer downtown to the county building where we will call on a number of departments who have requested information or a demonstration of a new item.

"Afternoons are generally reserved for cleaning up all unfinished projects, faxing quotes, looking for odd items that appear on purchase orders, and filing away POs and invoices. My day ends about the time that local traffic starts to build on the highway. This represents a ten-plus hour day, five days a week, four-point-three weeks a month. To say this is a hectic day is putting it mildly. However, if you enjoy what you do, it can be and *is* a labor of love.

"The most enjoyable part of my position is helping my customers understand their needs with respect to the use of the equipment. An example would be a customer interested in a laptop computer to do presentations at remote sites versus a client needing a laptop for communicating to his home base. One would need a CD-ROM, the other might only need a fax/modem. Some may need both.

continued

continued

"If I had to pick a project I least like to perform, it's the ton of paperwork that is a necessary evil in the day-to-day flow of business. The upside of my business is the satisfaction of being productive and helping others do the same. When I complete a project with confidence in a timely manner so my customers can enjoy productivity, I take a moment to sit back and breathe easy.

"The downside is always the fact of being in a race with the clock. I try to never let the clock win. I also refuse to let a discontinued product stop me from saying to a customer that I can fill their needs. Somewhere out there is a replacement part. All salespeople are part detective. We look until we find what we need to help our customers.

"For those who are considering entering my world, I would say to be prepared to plan for a very exciting career. Technology advances as fast as you can absorb yesterday's breakthroughs. Pick a school that offers the career path that you wish to follow (sales and marketing, computer network engineering, or service and repair). Attend as many seminars in the field as possible. Read as many journals that pertain to your area of interest as you can. Spend as much time as you can afford, talking to those around you in that particular field. Don't be afraid to roll up your sleeves and get your hands dirty. Ask a million questions. Experiment with the knowledge you've gained. Share your findings with others and never stop learning. That's my formula for success."

MEET JIM LECLAIR

Jim LeClair is the owner and sales manager for Advanced Computer Services, Inc., in Lawrence, Kansas. He earned a high school diploma and took some secondary accounting and business classes. He also has engaged in ongoing seminars and classes which are offered by suppliers to enhance sales, technical training, and product knowledge.

"I was burned out on retail and on working for others," he says, "so my wife and I decided to form our own business. She had a strong computer background and I had more of the business background. We felt our strengths would complement one another. Our company consists of training and network installations—from network design to integration, support, and fiber optics (to name a few).

"We have five employees. Our store hours are Monday through Friday, from 8 A.M. until 5 P.M. The atmosphere is as relaxed as possible, business casual Monday through Thursday, casual on Fridays. Our busiest time of the year is summer.

continued

continued

"I try to keep politics out of the workplace and am flexible with my employees and their families as much as possible. Overtime, for instance, is kept to a minimum.

"A day can change within the first five minutes you walk in the door. You have to be able to juggle things around to grease the squeakiest wheel. I generally arrive at 7 A.M. and leave between 6:30 and 7 P.M., spending approximately 30 percent of my time administering to the customers' needs; 40 percent working on sales; and 30 percent on day-to-day activities of running the business.

"What I like best is seeing how happy the customer is when we say this is how the network will work, and then the network performs as well or better than we anticipated. What I like least is having to discipline employees or contemplate lost sales.

"To be successful in this kind of work, it's very important to keep abreast of the current technology at all times, to be a good listener, to be flexible, to be able to read people, and to understand what they really want, not what they say they want. You have to be able to think quickly on your feet and have a semiaggressive nature. You just can't take no for an answer. Still, you must sell the customers what they want. Don't try to sell people something that isn't right for them, just because you can make some money.

"I'd advise those who are considering computer sales to be honest, to be fair, and to *always* do a good job. Our business has grown because we have gained the trust of both our customers and our employees."

CHAPTER FIFTEEN

PATH 6: OTHER COMPUTER SCIENCE CAREERS

"The real question is not whether machines think but whether men do. The mystery which surrounds a thinking machine already surrounds a thinking man."

—B. F. Skinner,
Contingencies of Reinforcement

 large number of careers are open to computer science majors. Even though many of them have been discussed in this book in detail, a number have not been covered due to lack of space. They include account executive at an advertising agency specializing in technology accounts, animation development coordinator, CD-ROM producer, computer book author, computer corporation media spokesperson, computer game animator, computer products project manager, computer trade magazine reporter, cyber café owner, cyberlibrarian, director of on-line service for nonprofit groups, freenet director, Internet access provider, Internet and World Wide Web page designer, multimedia producer, university computer operations coordinator, and virtual reality developer. And this list is not all-inclusive—the opportunities that computer science majors may explore are quite vast.

DEFINITION OF THE CAREER PATH

Computer Science Professor

> **HELP WANTED**
> University teaching professional with experience in teaching computer science or related courses. Ph.D. and research experience required. Fall semester. Local four-year college. Attractive salary and benefits included.

Large universities generally direct computer science professors to divide their time between research and teaching. Typically, that equates to teaching two classes a semester complete with laboratories and office hours, and spending the rest of the week working on ongoing research projects. Professors often teach a lower-level class, such as computer programming, and a graduate-level course, such as advanced software design.

As a professional on staff at a college or university, teachers must attend meetings, grade student papers and projects, mentor students, serve on committees, and attend school functions.

TRAINING AND QUALIFICATIONS

Becoming a professor usually requires a doctoral degree, along with some research and teaching experience. Educators may be assured of continuing employment if they receive tenure (usually available after approximately six to eight years of teaching and research work at that institution of higher learning). At top computer science departments, attaining tenure is extremely competitive. However, those who fail to become tenured at large universities may be able to achieve this at smaller schools.

Some schools stress research and publication, while others, usually smaller colleges, encourage professors to focus on mentoring students. Many professors cite the satisfaction they receive from teaching the next generation of high-tech pioneers. Other professionals are drawn to academia because of the opportunity it provides to pursue research.

Certain schools, particularly those with computer science departments, look for specialists, such as individuals who can teach artificial intelligence classes. In other situations, schools seek generalists.

Successful teachers must enjoy teaching and working with students with a variety of different backgrounds and interests.

Earnings

Salaries for assistant professors begin at about $40,000 per year. Tenured professors at large universities can earn $70,000 or more annually. Some universities have department chairpeople who may receive $100,000 or more per year. Not surprisingly, large universities and small elite schools pay more than small state colleges.

Professional Associations

American Association of University Professors (AAUP)
1012 14th Street, NW
Washington, DC 20005

Career Outlook

In recent years, securing a position as an instructor at a leading school has become very competitive. Schools have begun to seek professors with specialized skills such as a Ph.D. with an emphasis in operating systems. However, there are still many opportunities at smaller schools and at state universities.

Definition of the Career Path

Systems Integrators

Systems integrators are responsible for identifying and merging various technologies without disrupting the flow of operations. An example would be merging an inventory control system with a product database to maximize a company's efficiency. Systems integrators also identify weaknesses in current information systems and explore alternative technologies.

Working Conditions

Systems integrators spend most of their time in an office preparing the integration plan. A 40-hour week is standard. Overtime is common as a project nears completion, during installation, or when a design start-up begins. Contract work, perhaps including travel, is not uncommon, usually on a weekly or monthly basis.

TRAINING AND QUALIFICATIONS

Systems integrators need to have a bachelor's degree in computer science, engineering, or information science. Many have master's or doctoral degrees. These professionals are able problem solvers who enjoy analytical thinking. Excellent interpersonal skills and the ability to communicate verbally and in writing are also necessary traits.

Systems integrators often proceed through an apprenticeship and then work their way into an area of specialty.

EARNINGS

Salaries vary with experience, the location and size of the company, and the responsibilities of the job. Most employers offer paid vacations, holidays, sick leave, and health insurance. The median salary range for systems integrators is $32,000 to $52,000 per year.

CAREER OUTLOOK

This is one of the fastest-growing areas in the information technology industry.

DEFINITION OF THE CAREER PATH

Artificial Intelligence Specialist

Artificial intelligence specialists possess a unique and extremely valuable skill—the ability to program computers to imitate the thinking and reasoning processes of the human brain. These professionals have already succeeded in programming computers to do all of the following: make decisions, recognize voices and objects, interpret information, solve problems, and speak in a humanlike voice.

WORKING CONDITIONS

Artificial intelligence specialists generally work in teams with other experts, usually in research centers. Schedules usually include more than 40 hours per week including evenings and weekends.

TRAINING AND QUALIFICATIONS

These professionals must have a strong background in systems analysis or programming; or fluency in several computer languages. Most have at least a master's degree in computer science or cognitive science, which is an amalgam of psychology, psycholinguistics, computer science, psychology, anthropology, and philosophy. Many have doctoral degrees.

It's also important for artificial intelligence specialists to have patience, dedication, and the ability to work well in a team setting.

EARNINGS

Earnings vary depending on the setting, location, and specialization of the position. Most employers offer paid vacations, holidays, and health insurance. Trainees in artificial intelligence may earn $25,000 to $35,000 per year. Specialists with a master's degree may earn $40,000 to $70,000 per year. Specialists with doctorates may earn $70,000 to $100,000 per year.

CAREER OUTLOOK

The field of artificial intelligence is still in its infancy. Job opportunities are expected to grow at a more rapid rate than average, particularly because corporations are very interested in this form of technology. There is ample room for trained, talented newcomers to the field.

DEFINITION OF THE CAREER PATH

Data Entry Keyer

Data entry keyers are sometimes called data entry operators. They enter information into computers where it is stored or used for research purposes.

WORKING CONDITIONS

Data keyers usually work in offices. Since work hours may be long, these workers are susceptible to eyestrain from looking at video display terminals for extended periods of time. Back strain and carpal tunnel syndrome are also possible.

TRAINING AND QUALIFICATIONS

As a minimum, a high school diploma is required. Data operators must have the ability to enter data accurately at a specified speed. Employers often offer on-the-job training.

EARNINGS

Salaries may vary considerably depending on the type of company and its location. Typical salaries for entry-level data keyers are from $12,000 to $14,500 per year. Experienced data keyers may earn $19,000 to $21,000 per year. Entry-level data keyers working for the federal government earn $13,400 to $18,000 per year, and experienced federal employees can earn $18,800 or more per year.

CAREER OUTLOOK

The demand for data keyers is declining, although they will still be needed through 2005. However, opportunities are limited.

DEFINITION OF THE CAREER PATH

Technical Writer (Computer Software Documentation Writer)

HELP WANTED

The publications department has openings for senior writers. Candidates should have a Bachelor's Degree in Communications, English, or Computer Science, strong writing skills, and knowledge of data analysis or closely related software. Visual Basic or related experience also sought. For more information, please send your resume to Human Resources.

The Society for Technical Communication describes technical communicators as serving as "the bridge between those who create ideas and those who use them." With the wide proliferation of sophisticated products now available to consumers, easy-to-understand instructions are needed to explain how to operate such equipment. These instructions are written by technical writers.

Technical writers perform research and then write the instructional guides, reference manuals, and other materials that aid in the use of computer hardware and software. It is their responsibility to make sure that the documentation is clear enough to help the beginner and detailed enough to be useful to advanced users.

Technical writers must be able to convey the how-to information clearly and concisely. They must organize documents in a logical form and be able to provide good indexes to allow people to find the information they seek. They need skills and experience in graphic design, usability testing (do users really like your work?), programming, publications technology, and project management, as well as good attention to detail.

Possible Job Titles

Information designer

Product communications analyzer

Technical writer

Possible Employers

A vast number of industries employ technical writers, including chemical, pharmaceutical, aviation, computer, and electronics businesses. Technical writers may also be employed by research laboratories to write reports on research topics—anything from insect invasion to the search for a cure for diabetes. Federal employers include the United States Departments of the Interior, Health and Human Services, Agriculture, the National Aeronautics and Space Administration, and the Department of Defense (which is the largest federal employer). Advertising agencies; newspaper, magazine, and book publishers; professional journals; and colleges and universities also employ technical writers.

Technical writers are also employed by nonscientific members of the community, such as insurance companies, who seek to have their industry's terms and procedures explained. Other possible avenues for employment include composing booklets on employee benefits, writing stockholders' reports, and establishing policies and procedures for any type of operation.

HELP WANTED

Technical Writer
Technical writer wanted with a minimum 2 years technical
degree or equivalent experience. Minimum 5 years technical
writing experience in an engineering environment. Macintosh
literate. PageMaker experience. Familiarity with the telecommunications industry. Will gather information from engineering
resources and product managers to produce/write documentation regarding the following products: TRI-C, TRI-R, ACT banks,
U-BR1TEs, DSOs, OCUs, ISDN Net interface, and DDSTs.
Generate final layout to blue line of all artwork and text. Wanted
immediately with pay at the market rate.

RELATED OCCUPATIONS

A systematic and logical approach is vital to achieve success as a technical
writer. Similar skills are necessary for reporters, public relations specialists, and freelance writers.

WORKING CONDITIONS

Working conditions usually include a pleasant atmosphere in an office
containing high-technology equipment. Usually a 40-hour work week is
expected. There may, however, be occasional overtime.

HELP WANTED

Technical Writer
Our technical company has an immediate opening for a technical
writer. Compensation is highly competitive.

Duties will include writing, editing, and illustrating object technology documents and publishing them in HTML. You will be working
with a closely knit group of experienced writers in our communications group, so you must be a flexible team player.

Candidates must have three or more years experience writing and
editing technical publications. Should be proficient in HTML,
FrameMaker, MS Word, and Vision. Knowledge of object technology or software development is also helpful.

continued

continued

Technical skills should include many of the following: Multiple platforms and operating systems, UNIX, Windows 95, NT, FrameMaker, Word, PageMaker, Vision, HTML, Frontpage, PowerPoint, Excel, Exchange, Netscape, Corel, Acrobat.

With exceptional growth over the last four years and current commitments to implement enterprise-wide solutions for several Fortune 500 companies, we want to increase our staff without diluting our work ethic and professional integrity. If this interests you, please contact us.

TRAINING AND QUALIFICATIONS

Most technical writers earn at least a bachelor's degree—either in technical writing, communications, or English. Some companies require a technical degree with course work in book design and page layout. Writers will be required to produce work that is easily readable and must possess proficiencies in word processing and electronic publishing.

Technical writers usually launch their careers in entry-level positions, frequently as assistants to writers who have already established themselves. Assignments typically include updating copy and proofreading. Novices must become familiar with technical jargon and hone their abilities to confer with scientific and technical experts and translate information into simple terms. Research and reporting skills must be sharpened, as well as the ability to write logically, clearly, and precisely.

On a personal level, desirable attributes include excellent communication skills, the ability to meet deadlines and work well under pressure, graphic design abilities, and a good technical understanding of the systems.

HELP WANTED
Technical Writer
Our client has an immediate need for a technical writer to plan, research, and develop documentation including developer, system manager, and user guides. Must have 3+ years experience in software technical writing and experience using

continued

continued

FrameMaker. Must also have a solid understanding of UNIX, Windows NT, C/C++, networking principles, and real-time distributed computing.

Pay rate—$45,000 to $65,000 per year.

EARNINGS

Some technical writers are paid a weekly salary, while others are paid on an hourly or daily rate. Those who are on staff in a full-time position usually receive vacations, sick days, and other benefits.

According to a recent *Technical Communicator's Salary Survey*, median annual salaries for technical writers are as follows: entry-level—$26,700; mid-level nonmanagement—$35,000; mid-level management—$40,000; and senior management—$45,400. Technical writers employed by the federal government earn an average of $40,000 per year.

HELP WANTED

Technical Writing
We need an individual with 3+ years experience to serve as a staff writer developing End User Manuals. Candidate must have the following skills:

Strong PC/Windows experience

FrameMaker

MS Word

Graphics

Must know disk drive terminology

Must understand PC operating systems

B.S./B.A. or equivalent

Pay rate—$40 to $45 per hour.

PROFESSIONAL ASSOCIATIONS

Society for Technical Communications, Inc.
901 North Stuart Street, Suite 304
Arlington, VA 22203

DEFINITION OF THE CAREER PATH

Tape Librarian

> **HELP WANTED**
> **Library Systems Support Specialist**
> Our private university is seeking a computer professional to ensure service continuity and support the operations and staff using our state-of-the-art library system.
>
> This position also requires strong service orientation and excellent communication and organizational skills. Associate degree and computer skills are a must. The selected individual must be able to work flexible hours and weekends.

The responsibilities of a tape librarian include classifying and filing the magnetic tapes and disks on which data for computer use is recorded. These professionals also file computer cards and programs as well as various records such as the operating instructions for computers.

WORKING CONDITIONS

A typical schedule for tape librarians includes a 35- to 40-hour week in an office, usually near the computer room. There may be some overtime or shift work if working in large facilities. Tape librarians may spend a great deal of time on their feet while working.

TRAINING AND QUALIFICATIONS

Education and training for tape librarians vary, depending on whether the position is with a library, a data processing facility, or the government, but at least a high school diploma will be required. In some cases, positions will call for college degrees. People with experience in library work or data processing are preferred. Since each company requires training specific to its particular needs, on-the-job training is generally provided.

EARNINGS

Salary and benefits for tape librarians vary and are dependent on the size of the library and the type of business or agency. Most positions offer vacations, health insurance, and pension plans. Entry-level tape librarians earn about $16,000 to $20,500 per year, while experienced tape librarians may earn $24,500 or more per year.

PROFESSIONAL ASSOCIATIONS

Special Libraries Association
1700 18th Street, NW
Washington, DC 20009

DEFINITION OF THE CAREER PATH

CAD Specialist

HELP WANTED

CAD Operator
Manufacturing company seeking experienced CAD operator with HP ME10 or AutoCAD R12 or later. Mechanical drafting experience a plus. Send or fax resume.

Computer-aided design specialists are actually designers and drafters who use computers rather than pen and paper to produce their work. Working independently, they may specialize in a variety of tasks.

WORKING CONDITIONS

CAD specialists spend most of their time in offices working in front of computers. This kind of work over the long term may result in eyestrain and/or fatigue. Usually a 40-hour week is required, but overtime may be required when it becomes necessary to meet deadlines.

TRAINING AND QUALIFICATIONS

CAD specialists must have expertise in drafting and design. Though this may be taught on the job, most employers require at least a two-year program in drafting and computer technology. CAD specialists must be able to work well with others (especially engineers, designers, and architects), be able to meet deadlines, and have excellent communication skills—both verbal and written.

EARNINGS

Salary for CAD specialists varies according to experience and the areas of specialization. Usually, companies offer benefits including health insurance, pension plans, and paid holidays and vacations. Typical salaries at the entry level are from $18,000 to $24,000 per year, while experienced CAD specialists may earn $24,500 to $30,500 per year.

CAREER OUTLOOK

There is a mixed outlook for CAD specialists. Some say fewer CAD drafters will be needed in the future because computerized systems are becoming easy enough for most engineers, architects, and other designers to use. Others say CAD specialists may be in demand to develop new products. Eighty percent of all drafting is now done with the aid of computers.

DEFINITION OF THE CAREER PATH

Computer-Aided Manufacturing (CAM) Technicians

CAM technicians are employed in two different phases of projects. The first is the initial design and setup of the process needed to turn raw materials into finished products. The second is in operating, maintaining, and repairing computer-controlled equipment. CAM technicians assist engineers and designers who develop product designs and specifications, and help to determine the materials needed to make the product and the machines that will be used for its manufacture.

Working Conditions

A good portion of a CAM technician's day is spent in front of a computer. This can be stressful. Sometimes these professionals are required to work evenings or weekends (as there may well be a 24-hour operation at the workplace).

Training and Qualifications

Though a high school diploma is generally the minimum requirement for CAM technicians, most attain at least an associate's degree or complete an apprentice program. Course work should include algebra, geometry, trigonometry, physics, computers, machine shop and electronic training, mechanical drawing, and blueprint reading. Good communication skills and technical expertise are important along with the ability to identify problems and serve as a troubleshooter.

Earnings

Earnings will vary depending on the size of the company, the type of industry, the geographical location, and the individual's level of experience. Generally benefits such as vacation, holiday pay, health insurance, and pensions are provided by the employer. An apprentice CAM technician may earn about $14,000 per year, while an entry-level technician may earn $18,000 per year, and an experienced worker $18,000 to $40,000 per year.

Career Outlook

CAM technicians are needed in one of the fastest-growing areas in the manufacturing industry. CAM technology is increasingly becoming a requirement for manufacturers trying to compete in the international market.

Professional Associations

Computer-Aided Manufacturing International
1250 East Copeland Road
Arlington, TX 76011

MEET LINDA MIKULSKI

Linda Mikulski earned an associate's degree in general studies and an associate's degree in business management, both from Macomb Community College in Warren, Michigan. She has been serving as lead console operator at the school since 1975.

"This all happened because I was unemployed due to layoffs in the auto industry," she says. "I was majoring in computer science at Macomb at the time and answered an ad for an entry-level position I was attracted to. The position was in a field entirely different from the one I'd been working in. The monetary rewards were enticing and I enjoyed the atmosphere of the college campus.

"My position is anything but typical," she says. "I operate and program an environmental/security computer. Not a typical computer job, to be sure. I actually control the air conditioning and heating in all the major buildings on three campuses. I also monitor and control door security and fire security for these buildings.

"A typical day begins with a system check to ascertain what equipment is working and what conditions exist in the buildings. Because I deal with energy conservation, I'm responsible for auditing the amount of gas and electricity our power plants and buildings use. If, for example, electrical demand goes too high (causing us to be penalized by the electric company), my programs must reduce the consumption but must do so without causing undue discomfort to the building occupants. At these times, I must monitor the usage and possibly take steps to override the program, either to reduce consumption or to allow a building to run regardless of the consumption. Because computers allow automated sequencing of building fans (ventilation) without a human being present, part of my job is making sure the computer has the proper information. Special events must be accounted for—changes in basic scheduling (for instance, we tailor our start-ups and shut-downs with building occupancy, based on classroom usage) must be programmed or checked, and because we monitor fire conditions, part of my daily routine is to ensure the operation of the fire equipment. Conditions are very busy with the beginning of each semester but tend to quiet down after approximately four to six weeks. One of the things we do is take heating or cooling complaints from our clients.

"While my job isn't dangerous, since I control large machinery from a distance (one of our campuses is approximately ten miles from my location), employees who maintain the equipment can be endangered if they don't follow the rules and procedures we've developed.

continued

continued

"My work week is normally 37.5 hours, but because I'm a supervisor I tend to put in two to three hours extra each week. The atmosphere at the college is generally relaxed and friendly.

"We tend to upgrade our equipment every four to five years, or make additions to the equipment. With the computer industry changing nearly overnight, I have to learn a new system or a new method of controlling the equipment every few years. I feel this keeps the job interesting and it makes me stretch my mental abilities and awareness. I can't imagine doing the exact same thing for twenty years.

"On the other hand, some of the work can be fairly tedious, no-brainer type stuff. This is along the lines of data gathering and entry, most of which must be done by hand.

"Though the opportunities for advancement are limited, I am heartened by the fact that job security and benefits are very good. Among nonmanagement levels, my position is the highest. Lateral moves into the business end of computer operations are pretty much nonexistent. The type of programming we do is similar to business applications but has more specialized functions. Our department is small, myself and two operators. We cover three shifts per day, but only five days a week. We actually work for Plant Operations (maintenance but not custodial functions). However, we've been located in Campus Police because of the security aspects of the job.

"Though the emphasis of my job is on computer operation, I'd recommend basic climate control classes, math, and science to accompany the core computer classes. I've taken all of the above at one time or another and found them very helpful in improving my job performance and understanding. I've trained several groups of people, not just for Macomb but for Ford Motor Co. and for Detroit's People Mover. Those with knowledge of heating and cooling were the first to grasp the principals involved, though they needed more training on computers. Those with only computer experience seem to have a more difficult time assimilating the information provided by the program and therefore a more difficult time in arriving at the correct course of action."

MEET CHRIS SANTILLI

Originally a full-time company technical writer, Chris Santilli now spends her time as a freelance technical writer. She earned a bachelor's degree in journalism from Northern Illinois University and a master's degree in journalism from Syracuse University.

continued

continued

"When you're a full-time company technical writer, you're usually working in one industry, so you become an expert in one area," she says. "If you're writing for a medical equipment maker, for example, you become an expert on medical equipment. However, you become more of a generalist if you're given a variety of things to write: technical specifications, features, instruction manuals, instructor notes, and so on. As a freelancer, you may also get a variety of assignments—one day you might be writing about software, the next day you might be writing a procedure manual for a store that sells tires.

"As a freelancer or a company employee, you approach projects in pretty much the same way. You begin by meeting with the product expert—most likely a software, manufacturing, mechanical, or electrical engineer. Sometimes the product you're dealing with is one that's not on the market yet, sometimes it's not even finished yet. It is likely that this person doesn't speak English as clearly as you do—not that he or she is illiterate by any means, he or she just isn't able to communicate his or her ideas to the layperson. So you have to translate the 'engineerese' into more simple language. This means that you have to understand and know how to decipher the lingo. And you must keep in close touch with the expert to be sure that you are saying what he or she intended you to say.

"I work on a project for anywhere from about five or six days, up to six or seven weeks. I usually don't have projects that last six months, but many technical writers do. If you're going to write a software manual for WordPerfect, for instance, that's going to take a long time and involve many people. I usually work on projects alone or with one other person, so they normally don't take more than two months.

"Most people hear the phrase 'technical writing' and think of computer manuals. But in reality, you could be working for any place that creates any piece of equipment that needs to have something written about it—either how it works, what its specifications are, anything that needs documentation or details a procedure.

"When you are fiddling with a product, you sometimes uncover mistakes. Then you go back to the engineer and say, 'Aha, a little something needs to be fixed here.' It's very personally satisfying to find something like that.

"As a freelancer, you spend a lot of time working by yourself. Very seldom do you have contact with marketing people, but occasionally when you do you might feel slightly frustrated with their use of adjectives.

continued

continued

"There are many pluses to technical writing. The best part is that you work independently, making your own schedules and deadlines within the framework of the project specifications. Technical writing is very rewarding because as translator and educator, you are an important, integral member of the team.

"If you'd like to get an idea about what it's like to be a technical writer, here's some good advice. Choose an activity such as starting your car and sit down and try to explain how to do it in a step-by-step process. Begin the explanation from a point right at your front door. 'Step down the stairs, walk across the patio...' Remember, nothing can be left out: you must mention every detail. A technical writer needs to be obsessed with detail and accuracy.

"You really have to find pleasure in this kind of work to be successful at it," she says. "Believe it or not, during the summer you'll find me at the beach reading style books just for the fun of it!"

COLLEGES AND UNIVERSITIES WITH COMPUTER SCIENCE PROGRAMS

The following is a partial list of colleges and universities that offer programs in computer science. Currently, there are more than 1,100 four-year colleges and universities that offer courses of study in the computer field.

Alabama

Alabama Agricultural and
  Mechanical University
Normal, AL 35762

Alabama State University
Montgomery, AL 36101

Alexander City State Junior
  College
Alexander City, AL 35010

Auburn University
Auburn, AL 36849

Birmingham-Southern College
Birmingham, AL 35254

Chattahoochee Valley State
  Community College
Phenix City, AL 36869

Gadsden State Community
  College
Gadsden, AL 35902

Huntingdon College
Montgomery, AL 36106

Jacksonville State University
Jacksonville, AL 36265

Livingston University
Livingston, AL 35470

Mobile College
Mobile, AL 36613

Samford University
Birmingham, AL 35229

Selma University
Selma, AL 36701

Spring Hill College
Mobile, AL 36608

Stillman College
Tuscaloosa, AL 35403

University of Alabama
Tuscaloosa, AL 35487

University of North Alabama
Florence, AL 35632

University of South Alabama
Mobile, AL 36688

Alaska
University of Alaska at Anchorage
Anchorage, AK 99699

University of Alaska at Fairbanks
Fairbanks, AK 99201

Arizona
Arizona State University
Tempe, AZ 85287

Central Arizona College
Coolidge, AZ 85228

North Arizona University
Flagstaff, AZ 86011

University of Arizona
Tucson, AZ 85721

Arkansas
Arkansas State University
State University, AR 72467

Harding University
Searcy, AR 72143

Henderson State University
Arkadelphia, AR 71923

University of Arkansas
Fayetteville, AR 72701

California
California Institute of Technology
Pasadena, CA 91125

California State University
Los Angeles, CA 90032

College of Notre Dame
Belmont, CA 94002

National University
San Diego, CA 92108

Pepperdine University
Malibu, CA 90265

San Diego State University
San Diego, CA 92182

San Francisco State University
San Francisco, CA 94132

Stanford University
Stanford, CA 94305

University of California
Berkeley, CA 94720

University of San Diego
San Diego, CA 92110

Whittier College
Whittier, CA 90608

Colorado
Colorado State University
Fort Collins, CO 80523

Mesa State College
Grand Junction, CO 81502

University of Colorado
Denver, CO 80217

Connecticut
Central Connecticut State
    University
New Britain, CT 06050

Fairfield University
Fairfield, CT 06430

Southern Connecticut State
 University
New Haven, CT 06515

University of Connecticut
Storrs, CT 06269

University of Hartford
West Hartford, CT 06117

Yale University
New Haven, CT 06520

Delaware
Delaware State College
Dover, DE 19901

University of Delaware
Newark, DE 19716

District of Columbia
American University
Washington, DC 20016

Georgetown University
Washington, DC 20057

University of the District of
 Columbia
Washington, DC 20008

Florida
Daytona Beach Community
 College
Daytona Beach, FL 32115

Edison Community College
Fort Myers, FL 33906

Florida State University
Tallahassee, FL 32306

Tampa College
Tampa, FL 33614

University of Central Florida
Orlando, FL 32816

University of Miami
Coral Gables, FL 33124

Georgia
Albany State College
Albany, GA 31705

Emory University
Atlanta, GA 30322

Gainesville College
Gainesville, GA 35003

Georgia Institute of Technology
Atlanta, GA 30332

University of Georgia
Athens, GA 30314

Hawaii
University of Hawaii
Hilo, HI 96720

Idaho
Boise State University
Boise, ID 83725

University of Idaho
Moscow, ID 83843

Illinois
Bradley University
Peoria, IL 61625

DePaul University
Chicago, IL 60605

Illinois Institute of Technology
Chicago, IL 60616

Knox College
Galesburg, IL 61401

Northeastern Illinois University
Chicago, IL 60625

Northern Illinois University
DeKalb, IL 60115

Northwestern University
Evanston, IL 60208

Roosevelt University
Chicago, IL 60605

Southern Illinois University
Carbondale, IL 62901

University of Illinois–Chicago
Chicago, IL 60612

University of Illinois
Urbana-Champaign, IL 61820

Indiana
Indiana State University
Terre Haute, IN 47809

University of Evansville
Evansville, IN 47722

Valparaiso University
Valparaiso, IN 46383

Iowa
Drake University
Des Moines, IA 50311

Grinnell College
Grinnell, IA 50112

University of Dubuque
Dubuque, IA 52001

Kansas
Kansas State University
Manhattan, KS 66506

University of Kansas
Lawrence, KS 66045

Kentucky
Kentucky State University
Frankfort, KY 40601

University of Kentucky
Lexington, KY 40506

University of Louisville
Louisville, KY 40292

Louisiana
Louisiana State University
Shreveport, LA 71115

Tulane University
New Orleans, LA 70118

Maryland
College of Notre Dame of
    Maryland
Baltimore, MD 21210

U.S. Naval Academy
Annapolis, MD 21402

Massachusetts
Boston College
Chestnut Hill, MA 02167

Harvard University
Cambridge, MA 02138

Michigan
University of Michigan
Ann Arbor, MI 48109

Wayne State University
Detroit, MI 48202

Minnesota
Concordia College
Moorhead, MN 56562

University of Minnesota
Duluth, MN 55812

Mississippi
University of Mississippi
University, MS 38677

Missouri
Missouri Southern State College
Joplin, MO 64801

Montana
Montana State University
Bozeman, MT 59717

Nebraska
Peru State College
Peru, NE 68421

Nevada
University of Nevada
Las Vegas, NV 89154

New Hampshire
University of New Hampshire
Durham, NH 03824

New Jersey
Princeton University
Princeton, NJ 08544

New Mexico
College of Santa Fe
Santa Fe, NM 87501

New York
Columbia College
New York, NY 10027

Cornell University
Ithaca, NY 14853

North Carolina
Duke University
Durham, NC 27706

North Dakota
University of North Dakota
Grand Forks, ND 58202

Ohio
Ohio State University
Columbus, OH 43210

Oklahoma
Oklahoma State University
Stillwater, OK 74078

Oregon
Oregon State University
Corvallis, OR 97331

Pennsylvania
University of Pennsylvania
Philadelphia, PA 19104

Washington
Washington State University
Pullman, WA 99164

West Virginia
Bethany College
Bethany, WV 26032

ADDITIONAL RESOURCES

ACM Computing Surveys
ACM
11 West 42nd Street, 3rd Floor
New York, NY 10036

The Best Towns in America
Houghton Mifflin Co.
222 Berkeley Street
Boston, MA 02166

Byte
1 Phoenix Mill Lane
Peterborough, NH 03458

Career Information Center
Macmillan Publishing Group
866 Third Avenue
New York, NY 10022

Careers Encyclopedia
VGM Career Books
NTC/Contemporary Publishing Company
4255 West Touhy Avenue
Lincolnwood, IL 60646

Careers for Computer Buffs
VGM Career Books
NTC/Contemporary Publishing Company
4255 West Touhy Avenue
Lincolnwood, IL 60646

Careers in Computers
VGM Career Books
NTC/Contemporary Publishing Company
4255 West Touhy Avenue
Lincolnwood, IL 60646

Communications of the ACM
Association for Computing Machinery
11 West 42nd Street
New York, NY 10036

Computer
IEEE Computer Society
10662 Los Vaqueros Circle
P.O. Box 3014
Los Alamitos, CA 90720-1264

Computer and Electronics Graduate
Equal Opportunity Publications
44 Broadway
Greenlawn, NY 11740

Computerworld
CW Publishing, Inc.
375 Cochituate Road
Box 9171
Framingham, MA 01701-9171

Dictionary of Occupational Titles
United States Department of Labor
Employment and Training Administration
Distributed by Associated Book Publishers, Inc.
P.O. Box 5657
Scottsdale, AZ 86261

Directory of Directories
Gale Research Inc.
P.O. Box 33477
Detroit, MI 48232

Effective Answers to Interview Questions (**video**)
JIST Works, Inc.
720 North Park Avenue
Indianapolis, IN 46202

The Handbook of Private Schools
Porter Sargent Publishers, Inc.
11 Beacon Street, Suite 1400
Boston, MA 02108

How to Write a Winning Personal Statement for Graduate and Professional School
Peterson's
P.O. Box 2123
Princeton, NJ 08543

IEEE Software
IEEE Computer Society
10662 Los Vaqueros Circle
P.O. Box 3014
Los Alamitos, CA 90720-1264

Index of Majors and Graduate Degrees
College Board Publications
P.O. Box 886
New York, NY 10101

Information Week
CMP Publications, Inc.
600 Community Drive
Manhasset, NY 11030

LAN Times
McGraw-Hill, Inc.
7050 Union Park Center, Suite 240
Midvale, UT 84047

National Center for Education Statistics
"America's Teachers" Profile of a Profession
United States Department of Education
Office of Educational Research and Improvement
Washington, DC 20208

National Directory of Internships
National Society for Internships and Experiential Education
3509 Haworth Drive, Suite 207
Raleigh, NC 27609

National Teacher Exam
Educational Testing Service
P.O. Box 6051
Princeton, NJ 08541

Network World
P.O. Box 9172
The Meadows
161 Worcester Road
Framingham, MA 01701-9172

Occupational Outlook Handbook
Occupational Outlook Quarterly
United States Department of Labor
Bureau of Labor Statistics
Washington, DC 20212

Opportunities in CAD/CAM
VGM Career Books
NTC/Contemporary Publishing Company
4255 West Touhy Avenue
Lincolnwood, IL 60646

Opportunities in Computer Science
VGM Career Books
NTC/Contemporary Publishing Company
4255 West Touhy Avenue
Lincolnwood, IL 60646

Opportunities in Computer Systems
VGM Career Books
NTC/Contemporary Publishing Company
4255 West Touhy Avenue
Lincolnwood, IL 60646

PC Magazine
1 Park Avenue
New York, NY 10016

Peterson's Guide to Four-Year Colleges
Peterson's Guide to Independent Secondary Schools
Peterson's Guide to Two-Year Colleges
Peterson's Guide to Graduate Study
Peterson's Guides
P.O. Box 2123
Princeton, NJ 08543

Technical Support
National Systems Programmers Association
4811 76th Street, Suite 210
Milwaukee, WI 53220

What Can I Do With a Major In?
Abbott Press
P.O. Box 433
Ridgefield, NJ 07657

Where the Jobs Are: A Comprehensive Directory of 1200 Journals
Listing Career Opportunities
Garrett Park Press
P.O. Box 190
Garrett Park, MD 20896

INDEX

Academic assessment interviewer
  questions, 80
Acceptances, evaluating graduate
  school, 103
Accomplishments, listing, 35, 37
Action verbs, for resume, 28–29
Activities, listing on resume, 31–32
Alumni networkers. *See* College alumni
  network
Appearance, and interview, 77–78
Application process, for graduate school
  application review, 100
  catalog, 99–100
Application statement, for graduate
  school, 102
Artificial intelligence specialist, 185–186
Awards, listing on resume, 31–32

Bookstores, as research sources, 59
Broadcast letter, 37–39
Budget, developing realistic, 10–12
Business organizations, and researching
  careers, 57

CAD operator, 193
CAD specialists, 193–194
CAM. *See* Computer-aided manufac-
  turing (CAM) technicians

Campus employment services, 128
Campus visits, for graduate school,
  100–101
Capabilities statements, on resume, 37
Career libraries, as research sources,
  59–60
Career objective, for chronological
  resume. *See* Objective element, of
  chronological resume
Career outlook. *See* individual career
  entries
Career paths. *See* Resources; individual
  career entries
Careers. *See also* Resources; individual
  career entries
  researching, 44–60
Career-specific directories, for research, 53
Catalog, for graduate school, 99–100
Chronological resume
  action verbs list for, 28–29
  career objective element of, 23–26
  educational background section of,
    26–27
  experience section of, 27–30
  heading element of, 23
Circle of confidence, networking in,
  69–70
College alumni network, 63–64

Colleges and universities, with computer science programs, 200–204

College teaching, and graduate school attendance, 95–96

Communication skills, and follow-ups, 84

Computer-aided manufacturing (CAM) technicians, 194–195

Computer database manager/administrator, 114–115

Computer designer, 112

Computer engineers
general and specific skills for, 17–19
want ad example for, 109–110

Computer hardware sales, personal account, 178–180

Computer industry, demand for skilled people in, 106

Computerized job search services, 59–60

Computer marketing rep, 174

Computer network sales consultant, 170

Computer operators and programmers, 155–169
career outlook for, 166–167
career path for operators, 156–157
career path for programmers, 157–159
earnings of, 165–166
personal account of, 169
possible employers, 160
possible job titles, 159
professional associations of, 168
related occupations, 161
strategy for job location, 167–168
training and qualifications for, 162–164
working conditions for, 161–162

Computer product design engineer, 112

Computer programs. See also Software
for career planning, 59

Computer sales and service, 170–181
career outlook for, 177
career path definition for sales, 170–172
career path definition for service, 172
and cost-of-living index, 12–14
earnings of, 176
employers for, 173–174
job titles for, 173
personal accounts, 178–181
and personal values, 9
perspectives on, 15

professional associations for, 177
related occupations, 174
training and qualifications for, 175–176
working conditions of, 174

Computer science major, typical schedule for undergraduate, 123–124

Computer science professor, 183–184. See also Graduate school
career outlook for, 184
career path defined, 183
earnings for, 184
professional associations for, 184
training and qualifications for, 183

Computer science programs
colleges and universities with, 200–204
finding right graduate program, 98–102
graduate program information, 98

Computer scientists, 109–133. See also Systems analyst
career outlook for, 127
definition of career path, 110–111
earnings for, 126
employers of, 119
job titles of, 118
personal accounts on jobs of, 129–133
professional associations for, 128–129
related occupations, 120
strategy for locating job, 127–128
training and qualifications for, 121–123
types of, 110–118
want ad example for, 109–110, 111
working conditions for, 120–121

Computer service rep, 172

Computer service technician, 175

Computer software documentation writer. See Technical writer

Computer support analyst, 115

Computer technician, 172

Computer technology, in future, 107

Consultants. See Management analysts and consultants

Contacts
following up on network, 85–86
locating for networking, 63–66
setting tone for networking, 69

Conversation of significance, interview as, 75

Cost-of-living index, using, 12–14

Cover letter, for resume, 40–43

Database administrator, 115
Database services manager, 114
Data communications, 167
Data entry keyer, 186–187
Data entry operator. *See* Data entry keyer
Diary. *See* Experiential diary
Directories, for career research
  career-specific, 53
  employer, 51–52
  geographically based, 52–53
  job title, 46–48

Earnings. *See* Salaries
Economic needs
  calculating, 10–14
  and cost-of-living index, 12–14
  developing budget for, 10–12
  and monthly expenses worksheet,
    10–11
  and starting salaries, 12
Education. *See also* Training and
    qualifications
  and job selection, 44–45
  schedule for undergraduate computer
    science major, 123–124
  and underdeveloped skills, 20
  value of college/university, 122–123
Education section
  of chronological resume, 26–27, 31
  of functional resume, 35
  on targeted resume, 37
Employer directories, for research, 51–52
Employers
  for computer operators and
    programmers, 160
  for computer sales and service, 173–174
  for computer scientists and systems
    analysts, 119
  developing list of potential, 50
  geographically based, and
    networking, 65
  and interview process, 78
  local, as networking contact sources,
    65
  for management analysts and
    consultants, 137
  of operations research analyst, 150–151
  for technical writer, 188

Employment
  degree requirements and field of,
    196–197
  diversity of computer major, 64
  listing on resume, 27–33
Employment agencies, and researching
    careers, 57–59
Employment interview. *See*
    Interviewing process
Entry-level career options, exploring,
    20–21
Estimated monthly expenses worksheet,
    10–11
Executive recruitment firms. *See* Head-
    hunters
Experience section
  of chronological resume, 27–33
  of functional resume, 35
  on targeted resume, 37
Experiential diary, 16–17, 17

Federal employment offices, 58
Feedback, from network contact follow-
    ups, 86–87
Financial aid information, for graduate
    school, 103
Follow-ups
  to employment interview, 84–85
  feedback from, 86–87
  for graduate school application, 102
  on network contact, 85–86
Freelance software designer, 8
Freelance technical writer, personal
    account, 197–199
Functional resume, 33–35

General skills, 16–17
  in computer engineering, 17–19
Geographically based directories, for
    career research, 52–53
Goals, exploring long-term, 14–15
Graduate school
  application process for, 99–100
  application statement for, 102
  campus visits, 100–101
  as career enhancement, 95
  and college teaching, 95–96
  and degree program requirements, 99

evaluating acceptances, 103
field of employment and, 96–97
finding right graduate program,
   98–102
follow-up on applications for, 102
letters of recommendation, 101–102
motives for attending, 94–98
and postgraduate employment, 97
reasons for choosing, 93–94
rejections from, 103–104
researching financial aid sources,
   scholarships, and fellowships, 103
as "stalling" strategy, 95
Guidance programs, 46–47
Guidance programs, and computer
   science careers, 46–47

Head hunters (executive recruitment
   firms), 57–58
Heading, for chronological resume, 23
Hidden job market, 62
"Higher-level" needs, 14–15
Hiring process, 83
Honors, listing on resume, 31–32

Illinois, University of, and value of
   college/university education,
   122–123
Income. *See also* Economic needs;
   Salaries
   documenting need for, 6
   estimating gross, 12
Infomercial, as self-promotion tool, 67,
   68
Information resources
   identifying, 51–56
   locating, 56–60
Initial telephone job offers, 88
Internet/Intranet systems analyst, 118
Internships, 95
Interviewer, 79–81, 82
Interviewing process, 74–82
   and appearance, 77–78
   and employer information, 78
   ending, 82
   follow-up to, 83–85
   and interviewer questions, 79–81
   and lines of communication, 84

and questions about underdeveloped
   skills, 81
and questions for interviewer, 82
and references, 33
resume in, 76–77
and self-assessment, 75–76
strategies for, 79

Job descriptions, 48–49
Job offers
   comparing, 91–92
   deciding on, 89
   initial telephone offers, 88
   letter of acceptance and, 88–89
   negotiating, 89–91
   reneging on, 92
Job satisfaction, and personal values, 8
Job search
   career researching and, 44–60
   and follow-up, 83–87
   vs. graduate school, 93–104
   interviewing process in, 74–82
   and job offer considerations, 88–92
   networking and, 61–73
   resume and cover letter in, 22–43
   self-assessment in, 2–21
Job title directory, 46–48
Job titles
   for computer operators and program-
      mers, 159
   for computer sales and service, 173
   for computer scientists and systems
      analysts, 118
   for management analysts and
      consultants, 136
   for operations research analyst, 150
   researching, 45–46
   for technical writer, 188
Journal, in self-assessment process, 3

Lead console operator, personal
   account, 196–197
Letters
   of acceptance, 88–89
   of recommendation, for graduate
      school, 101–102
"Lower-level" needs, 14

Management analysts and consultants, 134–146
  career outlook for, 141–142
  career path for, 135–136
  earnings for, 140
  job titles for, 136
  personal accounts of, 142–146
  possible employers for, 137
  professional associations for, 142
  related occupations, 137–138
  training and qualifications for, 138–140
  working conditions for, 138

Negotiation, of job offer, 89–91
Network contact record form, 66–67
Networking, 61–73
  beginning process of, 69–72
  in career research, 49–50
  within circle of confidence, 69–70
  and feedback from follow-ups, 86–87
  following up on contact, 85–86
  general tips for, 72
  and hidden job market, 62
  locating contacts, 63–66
  obtaining information through, 61
  personal control of, 62
  preparations for, 63–69
  as proactive approach, 62
  questions to ask, 70–71
  record-keeping system for, 66–67
  sample questions to answer, 71–72
  self-promotion tools for, 67–69
  shutting down, 72–73
Newspapers, for career research, 54

Objective element
  of chronological resume, 23–26
  on functional resume, 35
  on targeted resume, 35
Occupational Outlook Handbook (OOH), 47, 127, 140, 176
  and degree requirements, 96–97
Occupations, related to computer science careers, 119, 137–138, 151, 161, 174, 189
Operations research analyst, 147–154
  career outlook for, 153–154
  definition of career path, 148–150
  earnings for, 152

  employers of, 150–151
  job titles for, 150
  professional associations for, 154
  related occupations to, 151
  training and qualifications for, 151–152
  working conditions of, 151
Organizations
  and interview process, 78
  as networking contact sources, 65–66
Outplacement (employment) firm, 58–59

Periodicals, for career research, 54
Personal assessment and career direction interviewer questions, 80
Personal traits
  considering in job search process, 7–8
  focusing on, 7
  inventorying, 6–7
  understanding, 3–7
Personal values, 8–10
  and acceptable working conditions, 8
  and associated values, 8–9
  defined, 8
  relating to career paths, 9–10
Portfolios, as self-promotion tool, 68–69
Preferred skills, recognizing, 19
Proactive approach, to job search, 62
Professional associations. See also Organizations; Professional societies and affiliations
  for CAM technicians, 195
  for computer science professor, 184
  for computer scientists and related occupations, 128–129
  for management analysts and consultants, 142
  as networking contact sources, 65–66
  for operations research analyst, 154
  for operators and programmers, 168
  for sales and service, 177
  for tape librarian, 193
  for technical writer, 191
Professional employment agencies, 57–58
Professional societies and affiliations, listing on resume, 31–32
Programmer/systems analyst, 117
Public libraries, and researching careers, 56–57

Questions
  categories of interviewer, 79–81
  for interviewer, 82
  networking and asking/answering,
    70–72
  about underdeveloped skills, in
    interview, 81

Recommendations, for graduate school,
  101–102
Reference books, for careers, 47
References, listing on resume, 33, 35
Rejection, and graduate school, 103–104
Research
  for career selection, 44–60
  collecting job titles as, 45–46
  developing job title directory, 46–48
  developing list of employers, 50
  exploring job descriptions, 48–49
  identifying information resources,
    51–56
  learning about work settings, 49
  locating information resources, 56–60
  networking and, 49–50, 63
Resources. *See also* Information
  resources; Reference books
  for career information, 205–209
  for cost-of-living indices, 12
  for graduate programs, 98–99
  about work settings, 49
Resume. *See also* Broadcast letter; Cover
  letter
  action verbs list for, 28–29
  chronological, 23–30
  cover letter for, 40–43
  functional, 33–35
  general skills described on, 17
  in interviewing process, 76–77
  and networking, 67–68
  producing, 39–40
  purpose of, 22–23
  questions resume writers ask, 31–33
  solutions to frequently encountered
    problems, 30
  targeted, 35–37

Salaries. *See also* Economic needs; Income
  for artificial intelligence specialist, 186
  for CAD specialists, 194
  for CAM technicians, 195
  for computer science professor, 184
  for computer scientists and systems
    analysts, 126
  and cost-of-living index, 12–14
  for data entry keyer, 187
  for management analysts and
    consultants, 140
  for operations research analyst, 152
  for operators and programmers, 165–166
  for sales and service, 176
  starting, 12
  for systems integrators, 185
  for tape librarian, 193
  for technical writer (computer soft-
    ware documentation writer), 191
Self-assessment process, 2–21
  and graduate education, 97
  in interviewing process, 75–76
  and networking, 63
  steps in, 3–20
  using, 20–21
  worksheet for, 4–5
Self-employment, consultants and, 139
"Self-managing" career skill, 15
Self-promotion tools, for networking,
  67–69
Skills
  defining, 15–16
  developing underdeveloped, 19–20
  identifying general, 16–17
  identifying specific, 17
  recognizing preferred, 19
  relating to employers, 17–19
Software. *See also* Computer programs
Software application developers, 113
Software design engineer, 113–114
Software designer, 113–114
Software developer, 112–113
Software engineer, 112
Software sales position, 171
Specific skills, 16, 17
  in computer engineering, 17–19
State employment offices, 58
Supervisors (present and former), as
  networking contact sources, 63–64
Systems analyst. *See also* Computer scientists
  career outlook for, 127
  career path definition for, 116–118

earnings for, 126
personal traits for, 7–8
qualifications for, 125–126
want ads for, 115–116, 119, 120,
125, 126
Systems integrators, 184–185

Tape librarian, 192–193
Targeted job posting publications, 54–55
Targeted resume, 35–37
Teachers, placement firms for, 58
Technical writer (computer software
documentation writer)
career path defined, 187–188
earnings of, 191
employers of, 188
job titles for, 188
professional associations for, 191
related occupations to, 189
training and qualifications for, 190
working conditions for, 189
Thank-you note, after interview, 84
"Tone words," 69
Trainers, 46
Training and qualifications. *See also*
Education
for artificial intelligence specialist, 186
for CAD specialists, 194
CAM technicians, 195
for computer science professor, 183
for computer scientists and related
occupations, 121–123
for data entry keyer, 187
for management analysts and
consultants, 138–140
for operations research analyst, 151–152
for operators and programmers,
162–164

for sales and service, 175–176
schedule for undergraduate computer
science major, 123–124
for systems analysts, 125–126
for systems integrators, 185
for technical writer, 190
Traits
employer-valued, 29–30
personal (*See* Personal traits)

Underdeveloped skills, 19–20
questions concerning, in interview,
81
Unethical behavior, reneging on job
offer as, 92
University of Illinois, and value of
college/university education,
122–123

Values
defined, 8
personal (*See* Personal values)
work, 9
Vendors, in computer sales, 173
Verbs, list of resume action, 28–29
Videos, for career research, 55–56, 59
Virtual organizations, 61

Want ads, 47–48. *See also* Career
entries
Work history. *See* Experience section, of
chronological resume
Working conditions. *See also* Career
entries
defining acceptable, 8
Work values, 9
Writer. *See* Technical writer (computer
software documentation writer)